A HAIRDRESSER'S DIARY

Christine Hannon

ISBN-13: 978-1475164282 (CreateSpace-Assigned)
ISBN-10: 1475164289

Dedication

I gratefully dedicate this book to David and Courtney--if not for them it would never have been written.

And to my dear husband, children and grandchildren, who taught me anything is possible.

Acknowledgements

Several people helped in the production of this book:

My son-in-law David and his daughter Courtney provided the support, editing and guidance, that made the book possible.

My husband Ron provided the photography and aided in the cover design.

My friend Betsy A. Riley consulted on editing and cover design, and formatted the files for publication.

.

Chapter One

For as long as I can remember, I loved fiddling with hair. My dolls may not have been well dressed but their hair always looked groomed. My mother would sit patiently for hours as I fussed with her hair. My parents separated by the time I was two, so from then till age six there was just my mom and me.

In 1951 when I was six, we had moved from Toronto to a small village in Ontario. Nothing, prepared me for what was ahead. My mother took a position as live in housekeeper for a family of six children, ages three to sixteen. Their mother had passed away just a few months before. We left Toronto, where we lived in moderate comfort and enjoyed most of life's necessities, to find ourselves, at an old farmhouse in the middle of rural Ontario. I had never seen coal oil lamps, an outhouse, or a wood burning stove before. Everything was different from how I was used to living. In this new place, I would come to know what it was like to be bone chilling cold, painfully hungry, unloved, and even from time to time feel hated. Those feelings would be my constant companions for me for a very long time. My childhood at times was to be a living hell. The eldest child, a girl, obviously resented my mother and me. At sixteen, she felt she could take care of her siblings on her own. Besides her there were her four brothers and a younger sister.

After just a few short weeks, barely settled in, it was obvious that my presence made things more difficult for my mother. There were the whispers behind my back, the threatening glares, and an outright refusal to try to be friendly with me that made my life sad. Apparently my very existence upset everyone. These acts convinced my mother to send me away to live with a foster family. This was the first of at least three separate occasions when I was forcibly separated from my mother. This first time I was only six years old. I was confused and terrified. I was taken away kicking and screaming. Begging for an answer I sobbed, "Why mommy, why are you sending me away, what did I do wrong? I promise I will be good mommy, please!" I pleaded, cried and clung to her; my arms locked around her legs, foolishly thinking this would save me. "Please! Don't make me go." My cries and pleas fell on deaf ears, and soon made her angry. The drive in the dead of night seemed to be very long. I curled up in the empty back seat of the car, not knowing where I was going or to whom. My sobs turned to spasmodic, shuddering movements, my body wracked as I tried to breathe. Tears stained my little face and my eyes were swollen almost shut. I finally fell asleep and when I awoke, it was day light and we where parked in front of a large, white, well-kept farmhouse. This would be my home for the next three months. Dragging me by the hand, my mother dropped me off, hugged me but making sure I could not cling to her. Then they quickly drove off. Fiery pain in my heart mixed with a paralyzing fear, how could she just leave me?

These dramas were short-lived, as each time, after a few months; Mother would come and get me to go home with her again. She acted as if nothing out of the ordinary had happened, as if she was picking me up from a vacation. Not even one word of regret. After the second time I did however grow to like the Secolds, my foster parents. Brenda and Jodie, two other foster children ages five and seven, became my new friends, and in a strange way my new family. There was always plenty of food, and we had all the necessities of life. That even included hugs and a kisses every night. The only thing I was unhappy about, was the abundance of turnips and parsnips. The Secolds grew them to sell, and fed them to us often. I grew to hate the taste and smell of those root vegetables cooking. That feeling still sticks with me to day.

Once back with my mother, hunger would set in again as food was not plentiful. I found myself eating sugar and oats left for the cows in the barn owned by the landlord. I was so young, and was so hungry my tummy hurt. I am ashamed to say that I stole leftover lunch items, bread crusts a half-eaten apple, anything I could from my classmates. I would find a reason to go into the cloakroom in our one roomed schoolhouse to see what I could scrounge. Burned into my mind is the memory of me eating almost the complete side of a chocolate cake, intended for a family birthday. This was a rare and special treat: spending the money to buy the cake ingredients meant doing without something else. After gouging huge hunks of cake out with my fingers, I turned the cake around, so the part I ate from was facing the wall. Finding the evidence the next morning, my mother angrily demanded, "Who ate the cake?" Of course, we all denied it. However, when told they would find out by the fingerprints in the cake, I tearfully confessed. No matter how much I tried to explain about how hungry I was, my cries did not protect me from being severely punished, being sent to bed for the rest of the day with no breakfast, lunch or supper. I was only seven. How does one deny a child food? When I complained to my mom about being so hungry, she told me the horrific story of my being one of a set of triplets. She said that the other two died at birth because of my greediness that I took all the nutrition from her body for myself. Now my hunger was also accompanied with sadness and guilt.

Chapter Two

Most of the fights my mom had with the rest of the family were over the fact that they did not want me there. To them, I was just one more mouth to feed. It was no secret that my mother was the lover of the man soon to be my stepfather, and had been long before we moved there.

I was tormented by the others kids in the family, but their actions were considered to just be games: partially burying me in the hole dug for the outhouse stringing me up over the back door with a rope around my neck. Luckily, my mother saved me just as the stool was kicked out from under me. Tears were my constant and daily companions.

Soon after I returned to live with her yet again, my mother became very ill. The family doctor came and was upstairs with my mother. I was downstairs hysterically crying and screaming, "I want to see my mom! Please, can I see my mom?" The narrow entrance at the bottom of the stairs was blocked, preventing me from going to her. No one could ever understand, the gut-wrenching fear I had at the thought of losing her.

Shortly after the doctor left, my mother came wandering down the stairs. I went running towards her with my arms outstretched. My face was wet with tears, and my eyes half-swollen shut. In a daze, and all flushed, she clumsily walked right past me, as if I was not there. Bending down, she picked a slat of wood up off the coal room floor, and started hitting me with it. One end of this slat had a small finishing nail sticking out, puncturing my body over and over again as she hit me. She mumbled repeatedly that I needed to be punished and that I was an embarrassment to her. I had blood on my legs, arms and bottom from the puncture wounds. Someone slapped my mother to make her stop. When she realized what she had done. she stopped, she grabbed me and held me tight to her as she cried, "what did I do, what did I do?" Sobbing uncontrollably I repeated, "I am sorry, I am sorry mommy, I am so sorry!" She bathed my wounds and covered them with makeshift bandages so no one would see. She begged me to forgive her, but it was not long after the wounds healed, I was off to the foster home again. This time I was sternly reminded that what happens in the family stays in the family, "Nothing" she said, "is repeated to anyone, ever." "Do you understand?" Nodding, I let her know I understood, but I was not sure I really did. This time it was three months before she came and collected me. Back to the place, she called home.

Chapter Three

The family was moving from the old, drafty farmhouse to a house right in town! None of us kids knew about the move until the moving truck came. This was a good sign right? I was going too. Everyone was excited, we would have electricity, an inside bathroom, and we would attend a bigger school. Out in the country we had been going to a one-room schoolhouse. Things seemed to have settled for a while. But the pace did not last long. Only two years had passed, when, at the ripe old age of nine, I was taken away to live with my Baba and Guido, my father's parents. My mother accepted three thousand dollars as payment for leaving me with them. This was to be my permanent home and my mother would come visit me when she could. This time I was not upset or fearful, for in their home I always felt loved. I had new clothes, a full tummy, and a hug every night before bed. Baba spoke broken English but that did not minimize that fact she spoke five other languages fluently. I would speak to her in broken Ukrainian.

My father, who was long gone, had no contact with them or me. My grandparents were disgusted with both my parents and one day Baba said to me, " Chrissy, he bad fodder, her bad modder" I felt safe, content and happy sure that I would never have to be afraid of being sent away, ever again. Almost on a daily basis Baba would let me brush and braid her long dark hair. When my aunt Jeanie came to visit, I would play with her hair as well. She laughed at my pretence of being little miss hairdresser. I missed fussing with my mother's hair though. Would she be coming to see me soon? Baba did not have an answer for me, just a smile and a hug; she knew of my pain.

Within a year mom did come, and wanted me to live with her once more. Baba fought for me, but my mom brought the police with her, they said Baba didn't have the right to keep me. Baba pleaded, telling them that she paid money for that right, but the police officer said, "Sophie you have no rights she is her mother."

I still remember that day so vividly. Still very young and loving my mom so much, I did not realize the consequences of telling Baba that I wanted to go home with my mother. I could not comprehend the lies my mother told, when she swore no more sending me away, no more hunger. The promise of letting me visit Baba and Guido as often as I liked was a lie. Her bribes of the Peter Pan and Tinker Bell dolls, finger paint set, and bag of candy, were just to play on a little girl's heart. The first time I asked my mom to go see my grandparents as promised she told me I had broken Baba's heart and she never wanted to see me ever again. Truly, my heart was broken--a part of me seemed to die. My only haven was gone. Deep in my heart, I could not believe it. It was not until I was married that I found out the truth. Baba's heart was broken that day, but not by me. She never ever stopped loving me. In later years, after Ron and I were married, we visited my grandparents and we saw the childhood pictures of me in my Baba's family photo album. One of my mother's neighbours worked for the London paper, and often had me pose for pictures that he submitted about our town. Baba had a close friend in our town who sent her all of the articles and pictures over the years, including the one of me playing a fairy in a school play. Baba told me she was always looking out for me, and I was always welcome to be with her and Guido. Sadly, I didn't know any of this when I was younger or I could have been saved from many years of guilt and melancholy.

Bouffant hairstyles over the years.

Chris with long hair, her specialty.

Chris' Poem

MOMMA

Momma! Can't you see I'm crying?
Won't you extend a loving hand?
Or lend a comforting shoulder,
Or hug me where I stand?

I crave for your motherly powers,
To wash away sadness and pain,
Putting your love around me,
Like an umbrella protects from rain.

Momma, do I love you?
I really cannot say,
Whenever I tried to show you,
You only walked away.

I'm sorry things aren't all rosy,
Or happiness, all peaches and cream,
But no one promised it simple,
And things can't be as bad as they seem.

So Momma; See why I'm crying,
Please, extend a loving hand,
Lend me a comforting shoulder,
And hug me where I stand.

Give me a chance to love you,
And I will try to understand.

Chapter Four

My mother had become more than just a housekeeper and lover, she was now the common law wife. Those people, the ones I felt hated me, eventually became our family. My mother suggested that I might feel more like part of the family if I called Art, dad. My last name remained the same, while my mother, of course, took his last name. No matter how you cut it, I was still the odd one out. It was pointed out how different I was from the other children. I looked different, talked different and had a different last name.

The foster family I lived with cultivated, sold, and served a lot of parsnips and turnips. Upon my return home turnips was one of the dishes served for supper. I knew eating it would make me throw up, so I timidly asked my mother to please excuse me from eating the turnips. Surprisingly, my stepfather told my mother to take them away. "Thank you." I whispered gratefully.

That's what made, the next events to unfold so hard to understand. Now that I was eleven, one of the things I enjoyed doing and was permitted to do, was going skating on Sunday nights. I wore my stepbrother's skates. With Christmas just around the corner, I added an extra plea to my childish prayers. Every night I would search the sky to wish on the first star in heaven. Before going to sleep, I said my prayers, asking for a pair of girl's skates for Christmas. Used ones would do. When Christmas morning came, and I spotted the big square box under the tree with my name on it, I got unusually excited. I could hardly contain myself,

In our large family, we had a tradition. One year the gifts would be opened the youngest to the oldest, and vice versa the next year. This year I would be the second to last to open my gifts. We all received one special gift and a couple of hand made or inexpensive items. We did not have the money to do anything else. I could hardly sit still in my chair; balancing the big, heavy box on my lap, bursting with anticipation. Time seemed to stand still. Under my breath, I kept repeating the same prayer, "Thank you God, Thank you God." I just knew it was skates. It just had to be! When it was my time to open my gift, shock and horror grabbed me, I felt sick to my stomach. There were no skates in the box instead it held a huge turnip. Everyone was laughing uncontrollably at my reaction. I broke down crying. Did I miss something? Were my skates still under the tree? Was this a joke? There was no special gift for me this year. When I tearfully asked my mother why, she said, "We don't waste anything in this house especially food and when it is put in front of you, you eat it." I had such a hard time accepting this hurtful, mean-spirited dirty trick played on me. Maybe it was all a joke, and I would get surprised after all. Broken hearted and crying, I had to endure the others laughing at me the rest of the day while they showed off their special gifts. When Christmas dinner was served my plate contained a heaping mound of turnips. I started to gag, and could not eat them so I was sent to bed without supper. I heard someone say, "She will have to learn." What I learned was to ignore the hunger; I was able go days without eating. Thereby causing an eating disorder that would last a lifetime.

I was very young when I realized I could escape some of my despair by writing poetry. I wrote my mom a poem, expressing my need for her to love me; she read it and laughed saying, "You sure know how to rhyme words." Somehow, the fact she missed the whole point did not surprise me. Exploring my artistic side, I discovered as well as writing, my love of drawing was also a passion. I found old papers or magazines to draw in. I altered the pictures of faces and hairstyles to incorporate my imagination.

Unknown to us younger ones we were moving again! This time, we moved out of the house into tents. We were too young to understand what part finances played on our housing situation. We needed two very large canvas tents to house the eight of us: six children and two adults. A smaller tent, would be used as a kitchen. The floors were made up of wooden planks and covered with tarps. These were pitched, in the backfield of an acquaintance, unprotected from the elements. Bales of hay around the outside kept the tent walls from flapping up in the wind. Bathroom facilities were makeshift. Inside plumbing was not an option. We were the talk of the town and the brunt of many jokes. Thank God this living situation was short lived, lasting only a few months. Wearing hand me downs was embarrassing, everyone at school knew the items we wore used to be in the donation bin. Small town gossips, a titillating group kept others informed.

Christine Hannon

On several occasions, two of my mother's younger sisters tried unsuccessfully to convince my mother to let me go live with them. My mother was the eldest of twenty two siblings nineteen of them were still living Being my aunts, they wanted to take care of me. They did not want me to stay in the unstable environment with my mom any longer. My mother and I had gone to them for sanctuary on many occasions before. These were the times she took me away with her instead of sending me away alone. My aunts were well aware of the family situation. Mom and I always ended up going back though after a few weeks.

Six months passed and once again, we as a family were moving, this time back into a real house, and thankfully to a new town. This town was much smaller than the last, bragging six hundred and eighty people, and I am sure that included livestock, or at least the Smith's two cats. Being new in town had its benefits: a fresh start, our past unknown to all. This was be the last time I would ever move with them as a family.

It was as if my mother was two different people. One person in public and another behind closed doors. Everyone loved my mom; all who met her, loved her. My new friends would tell me they would love to trade my mom for theirs. No one knew about my unhappy home life. A stern warning never to discuss what went on behind closed doors was preached to us often.

Chapter Five

I was now thirteen. My interest in hairdressing grew ever stronger. Babysitting money allowed me to buy books with hairstyles and other information in them. Most Sundays, Mom permitted me to go to the local restaurant after church. Some of the kids hung out there for cherry cokes, a treat I looked forward to. To my delight, girls in the town would ask me my opinion for help with their hair. It was no secret my chosen career was to be hairdressing. In this group, I felt needed.

Just down the street from the restaurant was a big old wooden bridge. Over the bridge, a narrow dirt path took me to a clearing near the calm, deep, murky river where I would sit for hours writing poetry. In addition, I enjoyed drawing pictures of hairstyles copied from the books; I altered them to look the way I liked. Dreaming I would be the one who would be styling the hair in those pictures one day.

In home economics classes at school, I learned to sew, and started making my own clothes. It was wonderful for me that

Mae, a woman that worked at the five and dime store, paid me with material and thread for braiding her hair.

By age fourteen, I was thrilled to spend my summer months working in the local poultry plant making my own money. We each had to pay rent at home, and that was ok because that improved conditions for all of us. Some of the women and girls would come to work with curlers in their hair, so at break times I could style it for them. I even got paid tips for that. I was saving every penny of this money, giving it to my mother for safekeeping. My goal was to go to hairdressing school when I turned eighteen. My mother convinced me to let her hold on to my hard earned, pittance until I enrolled in school. She said she didn't trust banks. I never suspected it was being frittered away. Beer was a staple in our house even when food wasn't. To help boost finances, my mom started a small home business selling cosmetics, I knew I was hooked. Hair and makeup. I knew that someday that was going to be my life. Of that, I was certain.

Hairdressing as a career was not readily accepted by my mother and stepfather. They thought that it was a waste of time and that I would never make anything of myself. They were also thoroughly convinced there was no money in the hairdressing business. I guess if I stayed in rural Ontario that might be the case. Not many farm wives strutted around sporting beehives or stylish coiffures, not on purpose anyway. Furthermore, I had never even been to a hairdressing salon, let alone seen a hairdressing school. My mother had always cut and curled our hair. The boys, on the other hand, did go to the barber. My career, as I imagined it, would not consist of just silver-haired little old ladies and tight perms. I wanted to style hair as I saw and read about in magazines and the Simpson-Sears catalogue. I was cutting my mothers hair by the time I was twelve. I learned how to cut and style my own hair early in my life. It is not an easy thing to do cut one's own hair.

I was proud of the way I took care of myself, and the women in the town often commented on this. They also mentioned their concerns at how overly thin I was. Having made friends with Gloria, the local hairdresser, I spent as much time as she would allow in her shop watching, listening and learning. She teased me about taking her business away from her when I finished hairdressing school. Laughing, I told her, "I did not want to work in small towns like this, I was big city bound." She just smiled and said, "I thought I was too. You have a passion not found in most young girls your age, so use it well." She added, "Go to school and specialize in what makes your heart race. You seem to be drawn to long hair, make that what you specialize in." After a deep sigh she said, "Here in this town you will be stifled-- there's no money to be made here, and no advancement. I do okay, there is enough business to keep me busy, but I will always be a small town hairdresser, no glamour, no excitement." These visits left me more eager and determined than ever to get started. Gloria allowed me to use her equipment on her hair so that I could become familiar with the tools that someday I would be using. She was supportive of my choices, and tried to convey the pluses of such a lucrative career to my mother. Not even Gloria could remove my mother's, small town blinders, so she could see the bigger picture. It was hard to explain how the scent of shampoos, conditioners, perms, and beauty supplies in the beauty salon was intoxicating to me. They were like an additive drug.

At age sixteen, after suffering another bout of verbal and physical abuse over the way I had styled my hair, I had enough. I was on my way out the door to sing as a soloist in church that day. My stepfather ordered me not to leave the house until I removed the hairspray in my hair; he accused me of looking like a whore. I did not! I mustered up the courage to take a stand for the first time, only to bring on a vicious beating which caused some very severe injuries.

Living next door was an OPP officer. My mother wanted to keep the family problems quiet, so she arranged for a friend to help us leave quickly in the night. We went from home directly to the hospital emergency room for treatment. My back, neck and arms, were covered with bruises. I had swollen vocal cords, which caused me problems with speaking. I do not know what my mother told them, but she demanded I be silent, she would handle it. I was just glad to be away from the abuse, so I remained quiet. We went from emergency to the YWCA. For that night, it was our new home.

Needing the funds now, I reminded my mother about the money I gave her to put away for me to go to school. It would certainly come in handy right now. Mom looked at me sheepishly, "Sorry Chrissy we needed to use that for other family matters." How could I have trusted her to keep my money safe? Why couldn't I have seen through her claims that banks were not secure? Without saying it, I knew in my gut, what the money was used for. Even at my tender age I could recognize the signs there in front of me. The weekly alcohol purchases, trips to the local bar, and goodies for company, the money for all that had to be coming from somewhere. I was angry, hurt and felt betrayed. I worked all that time for absolutely nothing! Now that I needed the money, it was gone and gone forever.

A Hairdresser's Diary

Like a lightning bolt, it struck me that the only person I had in this whole world was my mom. No matter what she did, she was all I had. I was petrified of losing her. First, my dad left, than my Baba and Guido were out of my life. I had to walk on eggs, but I needed to keep my mom happy, because she was all that was left for me. It seemed everyone I loved, someday would leave me. I could not drive her away too. Here I was in another city where I knew no one. I had no place to go and now I had no money. I needed to hang tough and I knew it.

My mother soon found us a small bachelor apartment in a house. It had a kitchenette, bathroom and living room, which seconded as our bedroom. It was roomy compared to the small cramped room at the YWCA, and a bigger place made things look brighter and more promising. During this time, my mother found a job as a waitress and I started to look for work as well.

Just around the corner from the YWCA I found a salon that was looking for an apprentice. I mustered up the courage to enter the front door walk up the steep staircase to and talk to the owner of Betty's Place. Betty was a middle-aged, soft-spoken woman, somewhat motherly but different from my own mom. She had very red hair in a mass of curls. Later she told me her red curls were an experiment, compliments of her son Billie's hairdressing school assignment. You have to be a great mother to let one of your kids experiment on you like that.

Apprenticing did not pay as much as a regular hairdressing jobs but the government subsidized it, which made the program attractive to Betty. This was a program to assist those wanting to learn the trade, who could not afford the schooling, so I would be there to learn as well as work. Betty said I could make extra on my pay check from tips, which was unheard of for an apprentice at the time —she said they would be all mine! The apprenticeship term was for three years. After that, I would take the government exam and be a full-fledged, licensed beautician. In retrospect, three years was not a long time. Nineteen or twenty years old was still very young to be starting such a career. Leaving Betty that day, knowing my life's dream career would start in this very place I was giddy with excitement.

This sounded like the best of both worlds: I could study in a salon and get paid. My mother was pleased, but said, "I was hoping you would find something that paid more." I shot back that if the money I worked for was still available, a better paying job would not be an issue. Yet again, she reminded me that in her way of thinking hairdressing was really a waste of time, and if I had a higher paying job it would not matter if she spent the money I worked so hard for.

For the next few days, things were very cool between us. She pointed out to me that I was doing what I really wanted to do anyway. "You are working in a salon aren't you?" She barked, "You should be less selfish." Adding, "Why can't you just be happy that we are getting a new start?" I felt bad and started crying, but decided I was not giving up my dream now that it starting to happen. Apprenticing for Betty meant I was being paid, so mom was not having to support us all by herself.

Our new start was short lived. My stepfather, the man we ran away from, showed up and my mother decided to go back with him. When I got home from work, she was already packed and ready to go. She had never once mentioned or hinted at her intentions to leave me here alone. Now that I was no longer a thorn in my mother's side she wanted to be back with Art. I ran out the door crying, as she yelled after me, "You can manage on your own now, you're a big girl." Returning to the empty apartment, I found a letter from her lying open on the table. On it was a list of the things that they were willing to do to help me. What was not there, was one word of caring or even a goodbye. First on the list, they offered to pay my rent for the next six months; giving me enough time to find a *better* paying job. Secondly, I would always be welcomed back home *when* this did not work out for me. They knew the poultry plant was always hiring, so I could work there again. Third and last was her explanation, in which she said, "The family needs and wants me back, and I need and want to be with them." She said, "If you loved me, you would not make things harder for me." If I loved her? What about if she loved me? So now, I was very much alone and scared, so scared in fact, that I was physically ill. Petrified, I realized I had no one to talk to or go to.

As I was working through what happened, thinking about what I had inside myself to get through this. I realized I had a couple of things going for me. For one thing I was neither shy nor afraid to talk to people, a regular Chatty Cathy. That was a plus. While I knew that talking to strangers was sometimes a blessing, I saw that at times, it was a curse. Not everyone was receptive to a cheery, "Good morning" or "How are you today?" Another thing that would help me was being able to manage on very little. The family had never known an abundance of anything, no silver spoon in this young girl's mouth. I had also learned to live on small amounts of food; going without for a few days was not difficult or unheard of for me. I had done it often before. Having this knowledge this made me a stronger person.

The next day when I went to work, I knew there was a fourth benefit as well. Betty. She was more than just my boss.

Not only was she my teacher, but before long she also became like a mother, treating me more like a daughter than an employee. Aware of the situation with my mother, she sympathized. Although she was not obliged to do so, she gave me a small raise. This money came out of her own pocket and I was grateful. I guess she saw this eighty-two pound, five foot six and a half sixteen-year-old girl alone in the big city, a girl who needed an advocate. I appreciated her acting in a motherly manner towards me. Betty helped me perfect some of the techniques I had already learned on my own. She never hesitated to compliment me when it was deserved. I was now in my glory. Finally I felt content and safe strutting around singing and humming as I worked. So much so, I managed to annoy one of Betty's customers. Agnes, one of her elderly customers had come in for her usual perm. I was singing along to some Ricky Nelson tune on the radio, and Agnes said the music was bothering her. I must confess I took my time turning the radio off, wanting to hear the end of the song. Knowing I was wrong, I apologized and promised to never be rude like that again. Betty smiled and winked, letting me know I had just done the right thing.

Betty's son Billie was going to hairdressing school already, as this was planned to be a family business. I was able to work with and learn from him, whenever he came into the shop to help on Saturdays. We hit it off right away and I so enjoyed listening to the stories he told about school. Experimenting with long hair was another thing we had in common, mading my enthusiasm for learning even stronger. He let me read his book of hairdressing, although I had a hard time understanding some of the theory. Billie could only help me so much, not having the instruments at hand to show me how things worked. It all seemed so complicated. As I tried to read the book, I was grateful this was not part of my lessons while apprenticing.

No matter what happened during the day, at night I was still alone. I wrote a long letter to my mom, being careful not to let her know how scared and alone I really was then I tearfully posted it. I did not want there to be any reason for either of them to claim victory. This was my life and I didn't want any negativity. From a dream to reality was my goal. Mom's answer came back to me rather quickly - I still have the letter in my possession. In her letter, mom asked me if I would come home, and sing for the women's church group on their special celebration day. I wrote back that I accepted. I hoped this would offer a chance to mend things with her. Singing in church could bring me some happy memories. I enjoyed being a soloist and my mother and I would often sing duets. I remember at one practice, my mother, who had a beautiful high soprano voice, was going to sing a duet with me. When she opened her mouth to hit a high note, and her false teeth slipped and almost fell out. I started to laugh and could hardly contain myself. She glared at me and shushed me with a look that said it all. I was the only one to notice but it was hilarious and after a couple days, she saw the humour in it too. It was our secret.

The ladies of the church were delighted with the news I would attend and sing for them. There was a wonderful turn out and I was the center of attention. Everyone wanted the details of my new life away from home, many made statements about my hairdressing position, and more than once someone would say, "We knew it! That is what you were born to do." Then again, "I knew one day you would be hairdressing." These statements did not thrill my mother. We did not mend our relationship on that short visit.

In London, I made friends and had dates but I was naive and learned the hard way to be selective about my choice of friends. Billie was fun, a platonic male friend. However, not every young guy that was friendly to me wanted to be just a friend like Billie. He and I were dancing partners - we both loved to dance. As often as we could, we entered dancing contests at the local London dance hall. We would do the twist and boogie to the latest songs, and usually walked away with first prize tucked under our arms. Billie was my protector and friend, the one who made sure none of the vulture like young men would take advantage of me. We loved horror movies and would huddle together when the really scary parts came on the screen. I didn't know why, but I somehow knew Billie and I would always just be very close friends. He warned me if he thought someone, I was considering dating was less than honourable. Sometimes he would suggest someone he thought I should date. Billie was very popular, but I was the only female friend he hung out with on a regular basis. I could confide in him anytime about anything.

My mother was sure I would get mixed up with an unsavoury crowd. Sometimes the choices I made were not the most popular ones but I knew they were the right ones. I chose not to drink, smoke or hang out with the kids who stayed out all weekend partying. I put my efforts into learning and after a while, those people just quit inviting me. I constantly, reminded myself that I needed to prove my mother wrong. One can only be told so often they are useless and worthless before either believing it or fighting against it. I chose to fight.

A Hairdresser's Diary

After approximately five weeks, Betty asked to talk to me after work. I was not worried, she told me a million times she was happy with me, nonetheless curiosity overwhelmed me. Betty told me that she didn't want me to work with her any more. Shocked I started to cry, "Why? What did I do wrong?" She put her arms around me and with a big hug said, "You don't understand hon. I don't want you to work for me anymore because you are wasting your talents here, and three more years would stifle you. I watch you and Billie, when he is talking about school the sparkle in your eyes lights up the whole room. You are too good to waste your time here. You need to be in school and with Billie." Panic set in: how could I do that? There was an aching pain deep in the pit of my stomach. Betty assured me there were government grants that would help me, and she had already made appointments for me to apply. Until the paperwork was finalized, I would remain working for her. It was hard to believe someone would go to such lengths to help me. Not being used to this special treatment showed in my excitement, promising her she would not be sorry or disappointed. She gave me a big hug and said, "I never doubted that for a moment." Once again alone that night, tears flowed, and I wasn't sure if what I felt was fear, excitement or both. I had been experiencing, such feelings daily in the very short time since leaving home, growing up faster than I thought possible.

That night my prayers included asking God to help me fight my fears, to make the right choices, and to stay on the right track to becoming a good, caring person, helping others.

Sometimes trying to please others was good, sometimes not so good. Trying too hard to please others sometimes made me sad. I was so afraid of disappointing anyone, especially those who supported and had such faith in me.

For the next couple of weeks, as the government processed my application for schooling, I remained working for Betty. To help me out further Betty, had a <u>Help Chris Fund</u> that would pay for items needed to start school. Customers put extra tips in a basket and on my last day, Betty presented the money to me along with a huge card signed by the customers. Overwhelmed with gratitude, we both cried.

Chapter Six

Today was not just another ordinary day; it was my first day of beauty school! My heart was pounding and I was visibly shaking. Unanswered questions flooded inside my head. Questions with no answers yet, except one. With extreme certainty, I knew that in eighteen months, my goal of becoming a full-fledged, licensed beautician would be a reality; much quicker than the three years apprenticing would have taken. This was the biggest single step to fulfilling my dreams. I loved the excitement this brought me from the very first day.

The unmistakable scent of hair products pleased my senses, the atmosphere and an overwhelming yearning to learn engulfed me as I entered through the large, white, double front doors into the school. I walked past the light-coloured oak desk where the school's superintendent, Helena sat. Looking straight ahead into the large room in front of me, I could see ten gleaming, white and chrome beauty stations, everyone equipped with a large oval mirror and a swivel pump chair, covered in turquoise vinyl upholstery and set on a chrome base. Above the mirrors were four bright, white, round lights, making the area exceptionally well lit. Beside all stations stood a black, rectangular, portable cart on a chrome stand with dividers for a variety of rollers and clips. No station was complete without a large ten inches high octagonal container fitted with a silver lid, filled with the turquoise blue liquid 'barbital' for sanitizing combs. Laid neatly on the top of every station was a white towel. On that towel was a pair of scissors, a razor, two combs, two brushes and a bottle of hairspray, and one of setting lotion, all ready for use. Attached to the corner of the station with a clamp was a mannequin head, covered with real hair, designed to aid students in learning a variety of services. On the shelf was a hand held mirror allowing students to show customers their heads from any angle. Walking through this huge room, I saw to my left yet another area. Through a large archway was a room filled with two rows of hooded hair dryers placed back, to back ten in all. Each seat was upholstered in a light yellow and turquoise floral pattern complimenting the chairs at the students stations. Once I had passed through, I turned around to take another look. I was determined to make it to this room this was the one seniors worked in before graduation. The last room I entered had ten shampoo sinks lined up back-to-back. These shiny black sinks were paired with reclining shampoo chairs in black leather, placed in front of them. Lined up on the high white shelf behind every sink was an assortment of shampoos and conditioners in containers. On the chairs were neatly folded shampoo capes also in black. Pure white towels, piled six high were placed above the sinks on the counter, next to them a box of tissue neck protectors. All other supplies were placed under the cupboards next to the sinks. A small, pantry-style room off to one side housed dozens of bottles of tints, bleaches, toners, peroxide, perms and neutralizers all placed in rows like perfect little soldiers. We had to walk through these rooms to get to our junior and intermediate classrooms, making this an everyday reminder of where we all wanted to be when we reached our senior classes. Everywhere I looked there was a sea of white uniforms and white shoes. The only actual color we wore was in our hair.

Everyone seemed very friendly; we were all there with the same goal. Some of us because we thought hairdressing would be an easy way to make money; some because without much schooling a trade was better than nothing, others like me was because it was in our blood.

Even the basement of the school was very interesting and informative. It housed a museum set up to teach us the history of hairdressing. In the far corner, sat a huge machine from the year 1928 that had been used for perming hair. It had wires hanging down from the top of a cylindrical dome. The wires conducted heat to brass rollers, which in combination with a solution permanently curled the hair. The solution used to make the curls was very harsh and damaging, but vanity out weighted the risks. The contraption looked like something from a science fiction movie, something used for torture, definitely not like a machine used for beauty. Against the cement wall was a long wooden table, lined with very old curling irons, these in their time were placed in hot coals or heated on a wood stove, then used to make ringlets or curls. These were Marcel irons, named after the inventor. A separate table held curlers made of rag strips with wires in the center. These folded over like a billfold to hold them in place once the hair was wrapped around them. There were wooden rollers made from durable hardwood and held in place with wire clamps. Weirdly crimped, twisted wires, shaped in elongated u shapes were used for hairpins. The collection even had an old-fashioned, heavy, bulky barber chair, which showed many years of service. Off to one side sat an antique hair dryer that looked like something from outer space with its large, oval shaped ridged hood. There was a full table of hand made wigs from the early 1900's, giving us a wonderfully dramatic look into the past. There was much to learn from the instruments and many interesting stories hidden in the basement, or as we came to call it, the dungeon of beauty.

When I started my courses, I learned that there were many subjects included in this school, that were not offered in other schools of hairdressing. Basic manicuring was taught in every school but not artistic manicuring. Facial and/or scalp massage was offered in many places but our course included full body massage. Basic makeup was common, but we had artistry and stage makeup added. Basic haircutting was in all schools but advanced techniques in ours. I took advantage of all these opportunities to the fullest.

My education was not just limited to just the classrooms but also included the teachings of real life in the big city. One day during the first week of school when Billie and I went for coffee, I mentioned that friends and family often asked me if all male hairdressers were 'queer.' I had no idea what they meant. Billie started to laugh as he explained it to me, asking if I ever wondered why he never hit on me when we spent so much time together, or why we were such good buddies or why his mother referred to me as the *female* daughter she never had? Until then, I thought nothing of it. I thought we were just good friends. I will not tell a lie: this shocked, surprised and confused me. Living in small town Ontario never prepared me for this. At first, I did not believe him. The things he told me didn't make any sense and I thought he was joking. Billie laughed at my reaction as if I cracked a joke. He assured me that our friendship was very special, but he was not interested in me romantically--only as a real and true friend. Telling me, contrary to rumours, there was only a small percentage of queer hairdressers in the business. They were there because of their creativity, not to meet women. I could not have asked for a better, more caring friend. We shared so much more than our hairdressing bond, even though he was almost finished with school and I was just starting. We talked about the wonderful things his mother had done for me. He agreed with her saying that when I was finished school I would be able to work anywhere I wanted; that my talent and flair was apparent to all, and it was obvious I was a natural.

Chapter Seven

You might ask how I chose this school. I did not choose the school, the school chose me. I was one of the students lucky enough to have my schooling paid for with government monies so I could receive my license. My work at the poultry plant during the summers paid off, as I qualified for unemployment insurance, and that helped pay for my school's tuition. I was just like many other students in other trade schools. None of our families were not in a position to help out financially. Therefore, while I was going to school full time, I also worked evenings and weekends to pay my rent, buy food and other of life's necessities. Sometimes rent and necessities won out over food, as there was not always enough money left over for many groceries. The need to buy school supplies from time to time during the courses also chewed up my grocery funds. I was able to buy some items second-hand, uniforms, perm rods, rollers. Billie gave me his used books, but some items like brushes, combs, and scissors had to be new due to government regulations on sanitation.

Christine Hannon

We already finished the first month of an eighteen-month course at Saul Popes School of cosmetology. This school taught much more than just the basic training needed to get a government certificate. To further our education which went above and beyond the required teachings, this school put aside one day a month to do hair for free, accommodating those who were low income, homeless or in need. Helena, our superintendent and the founder of the *free services to the needy* program in our school, made it her quest to reduce the injustice and shameless neglect of the homeless and poor. When anyone walked through the front doors of the school, Helena's warm friendly smile was the first thing they saw. Helena was in her late forties and small in stature her soft blonde short hair perfectly styled to frame her heart shaped face, her makeup professionally applied, displaying her student's finest work. When she spoke, it was in a voice, which commanded authority and demanded respect, but with softness and caring. This was a woman whom everyone loved and admired. There was nothing she would not do for her students, school, or customers, if it was in her power to do so. We were not surprised to hear Helena raise her voice in defence of her convictions when needed.

There were no frivolous services, like perms or colors offered in the free program. The school provided shampoos, haircuts, and basic nail care and scalp treatments. No matter what level of schooling we had, we all chipped in to help, never giving a second thought to services required. On free service days the school was closed to the public to ensure the comfort and privacy of the customers. Our clients needed help not judgment.

Marissa, our newest student, enrolled just in time to join us in the next charity work event. Having just transferred from another city as a first semester student, she was also the only deaf student to have ever enrolled in our school. Marissa and I hit it off right from the start. We found a way to work around the barrier of sound, and she shared with me that hairdressing was also her dream career. She expected it would be challenging, being a deaf beautician in a hearing world, but she was excited at the prospects. With a giggle, she said at least she would not have to listen to complainers. Laughingly I said, "That would be better than hearing your complainers, but not being able to see what they were complaining about." We closed our eyes making random gestures in the air with our fingers like scissors snipping. By now, we were both laughing hysterically.

We students now prepared for our day as volunteers. Enthusiastically, Marissa took the job of brushing the tangles out of each customer's hair, before the customer was shampooed. Throughout the day, our volunteer work had been going smoothly, we were working on the last patron when there was a sudden commotion around Marissa and her client. We all abruptly stopped our duties and watched intensely as her teacher frantically positioned a large plastic sheet around her. She received instructions, in sign language, "DO NOT MOVE!" Then Marissa and the customer and the entire station area where she worked, were wrapped in large plastic sheets and taped off from the rest of the surrounding area. To say the least, we were all intently curious, but after a stern warning, decided to keep a safe distance. For a few brief seconds the silence in the room was eerie, but soon the commotion and excessive chatter broke the quiet. We felt shock and confusion about what we had witnessed. With each passing minute, we became more curious, and were like little children who impatiently waited our turn at show and tell. Each of us tried to creep closer to the forbidden area everyone wanted to be the first to hear and see what all the fuss was about while still maintaining a safe distance. Before long three people, covered in plastic outfits from head to toe, came in and whisked both the customer and Marissa away. Her inability to hear or understand caused Marissa to cry, becoming visibly frightened and confused. None of us could truly understand or even imagine what Marissa's world of silence was like; so I plugged my ears with my fingers to help tune out the noise, thinking this would give me a small taste of her silent world. I was unsuccessful. I felt and possibly looked foolish. Soon after, several people from the Board of Health brought chemicals in and sanitized the whole taped off area. While we patiently waited for answers, our imaginations ran wild as we speculated on the many scenarios that would cause such a dramatic fuss. We found out later that the customer, had been living on the street for several years, and had not washed her hair on a regular basis. This enabled lice to infest, grow and finally take over her scalp and hair. Furthermore, sores and scabs from scratching her head with dirty unkempt nails had made the situation worse, especially in the tender areas around her ears and neck.

Learning about lice in class was mandatory but this situation was far worse than anything even our teachers had ever witnessed.

After that unforgettable incident Marissa never did come back to school; the trauma was far too much for her. She decided on a different vocation, one that she hoped would not include traumatizing situations. Was there such a thing? Even at my young age, I knew life was full of traumatizing situations. How we chose to react to these situations was as individual as we were.

A Hairdresser's Diary

I would truly miss my friendship with Marissa and hoped she would miss me too. It was very sad to know she would not continue to follow her dream. Each of us had to do what we thought best for ourselves, and we understood Marissa's choice. We all wished her well in her new vocation, whatever it would be.

After that horrendous and frightening ordeal, we were very cautious and the Board of Health ordered us not to speak to anyone about it. Lice was a taboo and shushed subject, although we were itching to discuss what we experienced. Ever since then, when we caught one another scratching our heads, we would make a rude lice remark. The Board of Health took on the responsibility to supply a place to continue to provide those much-needed free services. No longer would we do this as students, instead we would volunteer our time to the Board of Health. I was deeply disappointed that not all the students volunteered some were leery of working on the clientele the board of health provided. As things started to ramp up again we found that even more precautions had been taken we all wore rubber gloves and plastic outfits that totally covered our uniforms and shoes. Overall, we didn't mind and the patrons didn't know the difference. Being poor was not an indication someone was not clean, or didn't know how to take care of themselves. However, many could not afford professional salons services, so that is where our volunteers work made the difference. There was no recognition or extra marks, and many times, no thanks given, but we knew in our hearts that we really had made a difference, and that was good enough for us. After all, I came from a family that struggled and any extras were a luxury - I understood.

During our time spent helping others, there were many lessons to be learned. We witnessed and dealt with some agonizing medical and health problems. There was the mind boggling and shocking sight of a spider that built a web just under the scalp of one unfortunate woman, causing her severe headaches. The problem had gone undiagnosed by the medical profession, but was caught by the trained eye of our teacher. There were scabs and open sores on heads of men, women and children, from scratching with dirty nails or the sharing of unclean broken hair utensils. Sometimes these wounds would emit a sickening putrid odour. It was not unheard of for us to feel sick to our stomach at times.

We fixed jagged unprofessional haircuts on uncombed matted, filthy dirty hair that desperately needed grooming. One mother confessed to me she used pinking shears, salvaged from the trash bin to cut her family's hair. Lovingly, we manicured and treated broken and dirty fingernails, seeing that the torn or split skin where hangnails occurred, sometimes became infected. Our hearts went out to the people we were able to help, and I cannot remember any of us ever making a rude remark about what we saw. Did we talk about it? Of course we did. Did we shudder at the sight of some of the things we saw? Yes, but while we were looking we saw that we were blessed by the simplest things like the tools to stay clean, the desire to take care of our daily needs. I could not begin to fathom what life would be like living in such conditions nor could I understand how one could find themselves in such a place of hopelessness and abject poverty as living on the streets. Although I came from a family that was poor, even in my worst nightmare I could not see myself there. I did not expect to learn or experience anything like this when I enrolled in hairdressing school I was there to do hair. Nevertheless, what a gift, learning from a lice laden head riddled with sores what it meant to care for others. To my profound displeasure, anger and frustration, and to Helena's heart wrenching disbelief, the Board Of Health closed it's doors to the program, putting an end to the services so desperately needed by others, and so readily given by a few caring students and one superintendent who believed. To this sixteen-year old, the excuses concerning liability and safety were both flimsy and seemed deliberately uncaring. I could not understand why a country especially one that boasted caring for its people could be so indifferent to any one segment of the community. Making myself a promise, I swore I would be the next one who would change their way of thinking and restore Helena's dream. Much later, I would learn that this simple act, when shrouded in government regulations, would become impossible.

Chapter Eight

The junior class was focused on learning about the composition of hair, nails and skin. It was extremely important for us to know about diseases and problems pertaining to these three subjects and how to properly treat them. The last days and the lice fiasco proved the necessity of that. We would be using tools and products over the next few months and had to learn how to best utilize them. We would be taught proper shampooing techniques, with scalp massage, a facial, hand, and arm massage and a simple manicure. While not yet working on anything but mannequins, we knew these instructions were important, still I was itching to be working on live heads instead of rubber ones screwed onto my station with a clamp. Every day was a learning experience; sometimes exciting, but sometimes boring, especially when we had to repeat things over and over, but I could not conceive being anywhere else.

In my class, which ranged in ages from sixteen to fifty, was Dorothy, one of the older students. She occasionally invited me to her home for a family dinner, or at times to stay the weekend. She was more like a big sister and less like the motherly figure that Betty was to me.

These acts of kindness made it easier for me to remember to say thank you, but I still felt that was not enough. My humble poetry was pretty much all I could offer, and I did. The first time I wrote a piece for Dorothy, she cried, hugging me as she whispered. "Thank you. " Later, I saw it framed and hanging in the room at her home that would one day become her beauty salon. The poems became a signature of mine. Betty framed the one I wrote for her and hung it in her shop. Eventually, her clients would ask me to write for them. I wrote over 400 poems while I was in school.

Mrs. Kitchen was stunning a very tall, slim, well-endowed, woman with long, dark straight hair and huge brown eyes with golden speckles, she was one of our teachers who also occasionally worked at a local funeral home. She would tell us stories, some funny and some that made us cringe, but all morbidly interesting. One day during class, she offered to let one of us to accompany her to help at the funeral home. I was squeamish and not interested in joining her on one of her business ventures. Saul, who was rather tall with blondish wavy hair and quite handsome, our resident know-it-all, our God's gift to women specialist, stood up and very cockily said, "I'm not afraid, bring it on I will go." Mrs. Kitchen was delighted and with a wink to the rest of us accepted, Saul's offer to join her. For the rest of that day, Saul strutted around, boasting his bravery for what he was about to do that weekend. He boasted about how fearless he was, nothing would scare him! He called the rest of us scaredy cats. I did not argue. I knew I was chicken.

A Hairdresser's Diary

When the weekend was over, our classmates were all interested to hear about Saul's experience. Everyone settled in the classroom, but there was no Saul. "Where was he?" we asked. Mrs. Kitchen tried to hold back a soft giggle as she told us that even though she wanted to teach Saul about her weekend job, she also wanted to bring him down a peg or two. He needed to learn to be more respectful. She was quite aware of the reference he liked to make about her being so well endowed, and wanted a subtle way to let him know she disapproved.

She explained to Saul there where several steps to making the deceased look natural washing and curling their hair, or in the case of men a haircut, manicuring and makeup yep, even on the men. Each of those steps had to be done carefully, delicately and meticulously. She did explain to us that depending on how recently the person passed away, escaping body gases may cause some movement, to occur. Knowing what might happen, she asked Saul to start with a manicure. He picked up the client's hand, and as he did, her fingers lightly twitched. In terror he jumped back, knocking over the table of instruments and the stool he was sitting on. He started babbling, "Oh my God she's not dead!" After calming and consoling him, Mrs. Kitchen calmly explained again that there is still air in the body and sometimes these things happen. She made sure not to laugh, but she knew she had finally found a way to bring Saul down a peg or two.

It was two weeks before Saul came back to class; none of us mentioned the incident nor asked him about it. Not that we didn't want to! Especially those of us he had teased upon occasion, but we had promised Mrs. Kitchen not to. She was right. He had learned his lesson. The Saul that returned to school was not the same Saul who left two weeks before. He would always remain a know-it-all, but now not quite so cocky about it. It was also noticeable the way he now treated Mrs. Kitchen. Saul no longer referred to her as "Miss booby two shoes."

Pssst! Between us, behind Saul's back, on those times he was reverting back to nasty, a few of us would cup our hands squeezing them together in short jerky motions and mouthing. "She's not dead." And stifled our laughter.
He did not see or hear us but it made us feel better.

I started my intermediate classes after breezing through my junior term. Everyone knows the old saying, "Time flies when you're having fun" and my first six months flew fast. The mannequins were gone replaced by our teachers, friends and each other. Added were new risks, ones we would take with our live models; but we were still trainees. It was not until our senior class, after learning from experiences gone awry, that we would be qualified enough to work on paying customers. Thank goodness, we had teachers with ample experience to help fix the mistakes we would make in the next few weeks.

Our first assignment was to engage a classmate, one that was willing to let us experiment on them by bleaching, coloring, cutting, perms, makeup, massage and manicuring. I recruited James, a boy with lovely very dark chestnut brown hair, whose secret dream was to be a blonde surfer look-a-like. He told me how he pictured himself, riding a huge wave in Hawaii with sunny blonde hair clinging to his face, wet from the ocean water. Then afterwards, he saw it blowing wildly in the evening breeze while he rode on the beach in his light blue convertible. I could definitely see James doing all these things, and with his already tanned skin, felt the blonde hair would be flattering. But, before starting this huge endeavour, my teacher tried to warn us that his lovely very dark chestnut brown hair would not easily bleach out to a level that would be light enough to fulfill his secret dream. Nonetheless, being determined to make our teacher proud of us, and show our class how this was done, James was ready. I began by pouring the peroxide into the bleach powder and as I did the powerful, overwhelming, chemical smell took our breath away and made our eyes water. The mixture looked like icing; light, foamy and very white. We joked that maybe we should be in the cake decorating business. Ready to proceed, we both took a deep breath in and we started coughing from the fumes of the mixture. We laughed, unsure if we would survive. Both of us watched mesmerized, as his hair changed colors, clinging to a fleeting hope that he would transform into a blonde surfer idol. Unfortunately, he was becoming a Howdy Dowdy look-a-like. Jokingly, during the procedure, he said, "Well it's only hair; bald surfers might be an in thing." Still, I sensed a bit of uneasiness in his voice and that made me worry about what I had done. James' hair was now an unnatural color somewhere between an orange and lemon peel!! I began to panic, my heart racing and a fire building in the pit of my stomach. This was not how he was supposed to look. I did everything by the book. We stopped laughing and I worried.

Between the two of us, we decided to leave the bleach on longer, something that was not recommended by our teacher. After a few more minutes, his hair was straw-like and the color was only a little lighter, a lighter color of orange and lemon peel, the roots lighter than the ends. It was horrible.

Our teacher stood by, watching all of this, and did not once interfere or offer assistance. This was not my finest hour. I did everything I was taught. Other students came to watch and several unflattering remarks were made. My only comeback was, "Wait until it is your turn and we'll see how you do."Mrs. Steward, seeing how frustrated I was, came up to me and handed me a plastic bottle with hair color in it. I took it from her hands and shrugged. "What is this for?" I asked. She replied, "Just put it on his hair." Sounding a bit short, like it was something I should have known. As soon as she said that, James and I looked at each other. We said almost simultaneously, "How stupid." We had forgotten the most important step after bleaching the hair applying the toner. Bleaching removes color, toner adds color. James and I both gave a sigh of relief as his hair turned to a golden blonde right before our eyes. It was not as light as we hoped for in the beginning, but very becoming nonetheless.

This was not our only mistake over the next few weeks, but it was the one we learned the most from. James remained a blonde even after our fiasco, and trusted only me to be the one to keep it up for him. My favourite saying after that was "I'm only a beautician not a magician."

Next, it was my turn to volunteer to be a guinea pig. Until now, I had never been to a hairdresser. Only my mother and I had ever cut or curled my hair. I started watching students closely, to decide which one of them I was willing to trust. I wanted one of the new haircuts that were very popular in all the fashion magazines. Shaggy bangs were everywhere and I had not had bangs since I was a kid. I liked them and wanted to be the first in our class. I thought Evelyn was my best bet so I volunteered to be her model. Her specialty was going to be in artistic cutting. She would be able to create the cut that was different, one created with scissors and a razor, giving the bangs a very attractive shaggy look. Ready for the transformation, I was a bit apprehensive, but still excited. Evelyn was very pleased she was going to do a cut that none of us had attempted before. Everyone in our class surrounded us, watching as Evelyn made the first cuts with her scissors. Evelyn asked if I was happy with the length and I nodded, my head yes. As I nodded Evelyn made her first cut with the razor and sliced a huge piece out of my bangs. My long shaggy bangs were now a two-inch uneven fringe in the middle of my forehead. Evelyn had forgotten to put the razor guard on, protecting both her fingers and my hair from such a dramatic cutting mistake. I could hear gasps and see the shock on the faces of the other students. I heard one of the students say "Oh my gawd, what happened?" I looked in the mirror and horror spread over my face. I felt like I was going to cry. This was not easily fixable! Suggestions would have been appreciated but none were forthcoming.

The only solution suggested by our teacher, was to redo my hair totally, perhaps trying a new and wild color to go with my new and wild haircut. I was not so sure about this suggestion at first I had virgin hair, never touch by color, bleach, or perms. Nevertheless, with a smile and a new attitude, I decided to be a redhead; a vibrant, flame red with copper highlights, redhead.

Evelyn had no trouble changing the color of my hair; although it was so bright, I expected others would put on their sunglasses to speak with me. However, I was over-reacting. I could see it glowing like copper wire in the sunlight and it was not long before I grew to like the color, especially after receiving many compliments on how great I looked. The bangs, however, would take a bit longer to grow to an acceptable length and while we had a saying in school the difference between a good haircut and a bad haircut was about two weeks, in my case two weeks was an understatement.

Evelyn was so very apologetic about her mistake and jokingly I told her that one day I would get even. We both knew this was an empty threat. I held no malice towards Evelyn. Whenever we volunteered, we did so fully aware of the risks. Out of obligation, Evelyn volunteered to be my partner for the manicuring and make-up classes, ultimately the least risky of the remaining services. I began to question my own motives when I accidentally nicked one of her cuticles, causing a drop of blood to form on her fingernail. I felt bad, and was afraid she might think I was trying to get back at her for the bangs fiasco but she assured me she knew it was an accident, and was not the least bit concerned. I thought it would be fun to paint each of her fingernails a different color. After applying the burnt orange color next to the fluorescent green, we started to laugh. This was my feeble attempt to be Picasso. I painted designs on each nail causing us to laugh even harder, so hard in fact that the polish got on her fingers as well as her nails. Our teacher asked how we could have possibly used so much nail polish remover for one simple manicure; we looked at each other trying desperately to restrain our selves. The next task was the eyebrow waxing. Unintentionally, I made Evelyn's arches just a bit too high so she had a semi-permanent look of surprise on her face. Evelyn had never had her eyebrows waxed before so I was both surprised and relieved when she was pleased.

Theatrical and stage makeup classes were the most fun. Learning make-up artistry was turning on yet another hidden inner desire. There was no shortage of volunteers for these creative classes. Amazingly all mistakes made during these classes just washed off - no permanent damage or waiting period needed for the corrections. The males in the class were relieved at only having to take the theatrical makeup classes. They were not interested in the basic course; it was not something they would never use anyway. Using each other's faces as canvas, we each had our turn experimenting with color and design. Imaginations erupted as the guys enjoyed transforming us into Frankenstein, Dracula or in some cases the look of a high-priced call girl, but most times we looked more like clowns. Halloween was the perfect time for us to show off our newfound creativity. The girls in class were more interested in exploring the glamorous side of stage make-up. Even the most pitted or flawed skin could be made to look smooth and flawless. This makeup was not easily removed, a facial cream was needed and it made removal messy. But results were spectacular even if only temporary.

As students, we knew that we had reached a place of accomplishment when our teachers trusted us enough to let us work on them. We still made mistakes, some fixable some not so much, but learning valuable lessons was the whole idea. One thing that was very clear to me, was I still had a long way to go to becoming more than just a student learning my trade. Knowing I would not be a professional, until my place was earned in the working world.

Chapter Nine

At the beginning of my intermediate semester, I was involved in a car accident, which sent me home with my mom to recuperate.

Helena, out of the kindness of her heart, had loaned me the money I needed to take the train home once a month. One trip was special for me, it was during my seventeenth birthday. Spending it at home would be nice. There would be no extra celebration but mom would make a cake and as a little girl would do, I would lick the bowl and beaters from the icing.

My mother and I had an agreement, if I was able to find a ride back to London she would send me home with some canned goods, if not she would give me enough money to pay back Helena back for the train fare. No more, no less. On this visit, it was necessary for me to find a ride, as I was in need of the food items. Our neighbour the 'OPP officer's niece' Pam was visiting from London, and would be going back late Sunday night. She welcomed the company and I welcomed the ride. On the way home, it was snowing heavily and very dark out.

Unexpectedly, the car in front of us stopped abruptly, causing us to rear-end them.

Knowing that her young son was lying in the back window of the car I turned around to grab him and as I did that, the car behind us rear-ended us. I was thrown forward, smashing my knee on the dashboard. There were no other injuries. Thank goodness. I was however in shock and pain. Afraid of what was going to happen with her insurance, Pam begged me not to tell anyone about the accident, and after she dropped me off at the emergency door of the hospital, she drove away. How could I report her? I had no idea what her last name or address was. I phoned my mother from the hospital and she advised me to get the medical attention needed, and then find a way back home to recuperate. I had to be off school for a few weeks, my knee which was smashed against the dashboard and was bruised and the knee cap damage needed to heal and I was on crutches. The next day Helena once again, without hesitation, loaned me the money to go home. When I tried to explain I could not return her money until I came back to school, she shushed me and said, "How about accepting this as a birthday present?" Tearfully I thanked her. She even drove me to the train station herself armed with the homework I needed to keep up to date with the class. With me, I had a mannequin's head, a wig and a hairpiece including all utensils needed to practice.

Although I explained to my mother about what happened with the accident, and how I was left at the hospital alone, and the strange request from Pam to keep quiet, it didn't seem to bring much empathy. I suggested we talk to our neighbour and get the information we needed pertaining to coverage. Being injured I missed valuable time from school. The lengthy conversation between my mother and our neighbour did not include me, and the outcome was worthless. I was advised that if I knew what was good for me I would let it go. Once again, I had no options. Each day my knee got a bit better and I did my assignments faithfully. Going back to school was my only focus, nothing could have extinguished the fire in my belly, ignited by my will to succeed.

One evening I started an assignment. I had attached a wet hairpiece to the mannequin and clamped the head on the edge of the kitchen table, which allowed it to dry overnight, so it would be ready to work with the following day. The next morning the household, was awakened up by a blood curdling high-pitched scream, I rushed down only to discover my mother in tears, standing in the kitchen holding her chest and breathing in short gasps. She looked as if she had seen a ghost. I unintentionally neglected to tell anyone the mannequin was there. My mother, on her way to the kitchen, in the faint light of the morning, was taken by surprise. She was not pleased, and my extra heads were no longer allowed to be clamped to the kitchen table. Head and headless jokes floated around the house for the rest of the day, but were not actually appreciated by my mother.

A few days later, I left a bottle of a generic brand shampoo on the kitchen table, a caramel coloured, and thick, gooey substance in a clear bottle, which my stepbrother mistook for syrup, and poured on his pancakes. I was confused as to the fuss; it did not smell like, pour like or even taste like syrup, and had shampoo written on the side of the bottle. Really, it did not take much to figure out it wasn't syrup, and that struck me as funny. I realized I was no longer scared to see the humour in my family. Still, I took the hint that homework was not something I should take home.

After three weeks, I returned to London, this time by train. When I arrived at my apartment, my key would not work. The landlord's light was on so I knocked on their door and explained my problem with my key. They very rudely and angrily explained to me that I no longer had a place to live there. It seemed my mother had not paid the rent as she promised, and the rent was four weeks behind. They informed me that their constant attempts to contact her went unanswered, so they had no choice but to rent the apartment to someone who would pay. I was in total and utter shock. I could not believe my ears. How could that be? I was just home and she never mentioned anything to me. What would I do now? How was I to take all my belongings when I had no place to go? Then, as if a bolt of lightning struck me. Then they told me I could have nothing that was in the apartment, NOTHING! It was as if my heart was ripped from my chest, until the rent was paid, all of my things would be stored in their basement. Crying now, I begged and pleaded with them, to please let me have just a few of my belongings. I had only the clothes on my back and the homework items from school, in a brown paper bag with me. They answered me by closing the door. The pain inside I was feeling was like no other I had experienced. Please God, help me, please, help me! Then suddenly the landlord's door opened, but to my disappointment it was just to offer me the use of their phone to call someone to come and get me. I called the only person I knew that would be there for me, Billie. After making my phone call, I was invited, to go outside and sit on the porch and wait, quietly. It was nine thirty and they didn't want their tenants to be disturbed. What seemed like hours was in reality only a few minutes and then Billie was there. I cried once again on his shoulder, and he assured me it would be all right. He told me his mother had a friend who owned a girls boarding house and she was expecting me. That night I spent the first night of a very long stay in the boarding house of Aunt J. Wearing borrowed clothes, I resumed my schooling the next day. Speaking to my mother about the rent situation, only brought more lies, and with that strength I didn't know I had. I made a decision. A decision which changed me. I knew I no longer needed or wanted the help from my mother. I now depended on myself. Billie was surprisingly pleased. I was back to the hand-me-down donation bins, and for that I was grateful. I would never see my belongings again I was informed later. When I tried to retrieve them by taking a police officer with me, I was informed that they sold what they could, the rest they threw away. How was that justice or even humane? I was only seventeen. My whole life had been in those few boxes. After a few shed tears, I thought, oh well another lesson learned. I would have to start fresh and I did.

Chapter Ten

Desperately, I needed a part time job. Bob's House of Beauty was just around the corner and he was in need of a shampoo girl and assistant. I applied for the position and Bob hired me to start immediately. Now I was attending school full time and working Thursday nights, Friday nights and Saturdays, which kept me on tenterhooks.

Bob's House of Beauty was a laid-back place to work. His customers were friendly and we had a lot of fun. I met the person who became my oldest and dearest friend at Bob's. Marylou was just a couple of years older than I was and already married. She used to tease me about my flame red hair, referring to me as the red headed Q-tip whirling into the shop and whirling out again. She jokingly would say one could always hear me even if you could not see me. I was neither timid nor shy.

Situated in East London, Bob's shop had a large walk in clientele. One afternoon Bob, was approached by a customer who wanted a full body bleaching. That was truly weird and when Bob got over the shock of the request, he declined. It seemed this customer had customers of her own that preferred blondes and wanted to accommodate them. At first she was not going to take no for an answer but finally got the message. "This is one" Bob confessed "for the books I have never been asked that before." Bob had more fun trying to explain to me why this customer wanted his service than anything. This was how I was introduced to what prostitution was and I was speechless, a rare occasion indeed. I was never bored working at Bob's.

I learned very quickly, that hairdressers are subconsciously thought of, as everyone's shoulder to cry on, everyone's sympathetic ear, the keepers of secrets, and the builders of egos but most of all miracle workers. My training taught me to be professional, prompt, courteous, polite, and caring, a good listener, but most of all discreet. We hold a lot of power in our hands and most do not realize just how much power we have. For those of us that take it seriously, we make sure we handle that power with kid gloves. It is obvious to me that we are the unpaid psychologists of the world. We hear it all, see it all, share it all and are expected to help solve it all. This is not something we were taught or planned for just something that happens. There are things clients tell us they don't even tell their best friends. I often wondered if working on someone's head loosened their tongues. I, for one, heard things I wish I had not. On the other hand, I was able to point customers in the right direction to get the help they needed.

When we were not too busy in the shop Bob encouraged me to cut and style some of his friends and family's hair. We both knew until I was licensed I was not allowed to work on paying customers, as it was a liability issue. Bob wanted me to get used to doing more than just shampooing and clean up. He said that my passion did not go unnoticed and he wanted to help cultivate it.

Anna, a sweet frail little old lady that came into the shop every other Thursday evening was a special customer and friend of Bobs. Bob met her at the door when she rode up. He would go out, pick her up, and carry her into the shop. I always took care to be very gentle while shampooing her hair. She always had a smile and thank you for me. One day she lightly patted me on the face saying, "You're a very sweet little girl." Bob Picked her up again, she wrapped her arms around his neck and laid her head against his cheek, like a little girl. Gently he placed her in the chair at his station. After he styled her hair and fussed over her for a couple of hours, he would carefully carry her back outside and set her into her wheelchair just outside the front door. Her daughter waited in the restaurant next door and when she watched Bob set her mother down, she came out giving him a big bear hug before taking her mom home. This dear soul was the best friend of Bob's deceased mother. I once asked Bob why the client's daughter never came into the shop with her and said, "They live together and this is their alone time." It was not long after that her weekly visits stopped. I did not ask.

Chapter Eleven

Billie who had now graduated, and was working in his mother's salon, was coming to me for his haircuts. It was obvious he missed school and the fun we had. I was not yet permitted to work on paying customers, but Billie was a friend and volunteer so that was acceptable. We discussed how great it would be working with him and his mother after I finished school. Billie relayed a message from the elderly lady, that I so rudely upset while I listened to Ricky Nelson, when I worked at Betty's salon. She asked him to tell me, the skinny fireball made her smile.

Styling long hair over any other length was my preference. Incorporating curls with braids to create a masterpiece was very satisfying, mastering a beehive style that took a lot of precise designing, back combing and spray took lots of creativity. We had styling contests at school, and I won hands down every time. I, became well known for being a long hair stylist and even though paying customers requested me, as an intermediate I was not allowed to work on them. Those were the government's rules and the risk of losing everything I worked for up until now was not realistic. Secretly though, it would have been wonderful to get my hands into some of the heads of hair that came through the door each day. Inexpensive prices guaranteed a great deal of both regulars and walk in clientele. These clients had to sign a waiver of liability releasing the student, teacher or school from responsibility for any mistake or faux pas. This was for everyone's protection

I loved working with the customers, from a mixture of various ethnic groups. We had very few African Canadian customers; as our training was limited to do scalp treatment, waxing, manicures or pedicures only. Special techniques and training was needed for straightening, conditioning and cutting hair originating from the African continent. This knowledge was something only obtained while I was out in the working world. There was an ocean of experience only acquired when we worked hands on, in the everyday workplace. The knowledge we gained in school, was just the ice tip of what we would finally use to build our careers. In some cases, the customer would be our best teacher as they shared their knowledge and experiences. Closing ones mind to any information no matter how unimportant it seemed at the time would be a vast mistake. Therefore, I listened, watched and learned. In time I would be able to successfully accommodate all hair types.

Meg and Jeannie's Modeling Studio was a famous well-known modeling agency, located on the top floor of the school. Only paying students taking Megs and Jeannie's modeling course were usually allowed upstairs. It was no secret the course, was very expensive and none of the courses, offered by the government program I benefited from covered it. I envied some of the glamorous portraits that hung at the bottom of the staircase. I wished someday one might be of me. Our senior classes were responsible for most of the styles and makeup applications in those pictures, and that gave me a feeling of pride. Therefore, when Meg requested my presence in her office, I was both surprised and definitely curious.

Meg said she had watched me for a quite a while and admired the way I carried myself, she noted I walked with poise and confidence. Little did she know that my confidence was only cosmetic I did not feel that inside of me. Meg discovered that she was one model short for a Simpson Sears catalogue booking, so she asked if I would be interested in helping her with her dilemma. This was an amazing opportunity. So without hesitation, I accepted. I was afraid to pass up what was to me the chance of a lifetime. Although, I was somewhat concerned about my lack of training. She assured me that my a five foot six and a half inch tall, eighty two pound frame and great posture was all that was required for this assignment. A short lesson on what she called 'strutting the runway' was the only training I needed.

My grandmother - and mothers mom - was the one who deserved the credit for the way I walked and stood. Grandmother was the mother of twenty-two children. She was slim and walked poker straight with perfect posture. When she caught me slouching even a little she would run her thumbnail up my back saying "Christine, shoulders back and head up high." I dutifully followed her grandmotherly advice and now it would pay off.

Meg offered me her modeling course free as compensation for being available as an occasional fill in for her overbooked schedule. My payment for this would be not be money but instead, specially designed clothes made to fit only me, and her free certified modeling course. I had never owned a designer anything, let alone an outfit custom designed just for me. This was intriguing, exciting and a dream come true. Who would not jump at this chance? My career now would include modeling as well. Amazing!

Sometimes while alone I would try to make sense out of what had happened in my life. Could my mother and stepfather have been so wrong all these years? Did other people see me differently than they did? Never did I doubt my choices. I knew they were the right ones and that I made a significant difference.

I learned very early on, that styling someone's hair and applying makeup would and could make the world of difference in someone's self-esteem. Having the talent to bring that good feeling to others was rewarding on so many levels. It was a rush for me when a customer fussed over how I made him or her look and feel. Hairdressing never felt like work to me and the challenges only made me better at what I knew I was born to do.

Our class was a very close-knit group and we spent all of our school time together, including lunches and breaks. We were so close in fact that for my eighteenth birthday the students had a birthday party for me in our classroom. I had never had a birthday party before. I cannot even describe the emotions my heart felt that day. Even the two classmates that didn't like my sense of humour or my giddiness, helped me celebrate. One day Helena and I had a heart to heart about my fighting spirit. She said, "You are like a tightly packed firecracker, ready to burst into a wild, bright, flaming spray of multi colors." She added. "It is as if you are a wind up doll all wound up." As I stated before I was a regular Chatty Cathy. Helena said she had noticed that a couple of my classmates, found me overwhelming and obnoxious, while the majority found me funny, happy, and my witty personality contagious. She wanted to impress on me, the importance, of not changing the person I was, to please the few, who found I did not fit in to their niche. We discussed how I was so different from all of the family members I grew up with, including my mother. She hinted that my way of dealing with my painful childhood could very well be through my humour and my bubbly nature. Adding "That is a wonderful thing Chris, there is no shame in being the class clown when it has brought so much laughter and joy to us." I shared with Helena the heart wrenching fear I had of becoming like my mother and my desperate need to prove myself. In a soft voice she said, "Chris I am going to tell you something you don't know, you are a loving, caring, giving and happy person. God has given you a great many obstacles and you have knocked everyone down with a mighty push," Finishing she conclude with, "And we all love you for it." It was at that, very minute, that I felt like I truly made a difference. I had grown so much in the last years.

Chapter Twelve

We from Saul Popes frequented a small restaurant across the alley from school. We walked through the kitchen of the restaurant to the front where we would meet. This is how I met Ron. He worked for an optometrist, right next door to the school and went to the same restaurant using the same route. His quiet, shy demeanour and good looks grabbed my attention immediately. I however could not let his shyness go unnoticed without a cute comment. So one day when a group of us girls were going for lunch, I saw Ron was standing at the back door of his work place and I could not help myself, I looked at him and said, "Well if it isn't my little lover." We laughed as we all skipped off giggling. Ron, hopped down off the back step and followed us into the restaurant. It was only a couple weeks later that we started dating. Once we did, we spent every available minute we could together seven days a week. Ron who was the ripe old age of eighteen lived at home with his parents and family, a normal, happy, close family. Soon after we met, it was obvious to those who knew us we would be partners for the rest of our lives. He supported my choices of modeling as well as hairdressing. Prepared to face the world head on alone, no longer would be my destiny; I now had someone to share it with. Love was something my heart yearned to experience, unconditional, unshared, true love. Part of me was afraid to let him love me I was famous for losing the people I loved. Ron assured me his feelings for me were not throw away. I had never experienced happiness, love or contentment like I did with Ron.

I wanted to share this wonderful news with Betty, Billie and my mother and the plan to have them meet Ron, was exciting. So far, the most I had shared with my mother about Ron was I had been dating him. I had not returned home since the last incident so we communicated only by mail. Ron proposed to me after five months of dating and in the same ally we frequented so often on our trips back and forth from school, his work place and the restaurant. Until I graduated, we would be side by side in our respective positions.

The modeling portion of my career took second place to my hairdressing, although I posed for catalogues, magazines, hair shows and did runway work I somehow found the necessary time. The focus was usually on headshots or my long shapely legs and my eighteen-inch waist. The whirlwind pace, respect, recognition and the gorgeous designer clothes were just a few of the things that made this career exciting.

There would many more surprises in store for me, some pleasant but in this one case extremely upsetting. Unemployment insurance had contacted the school advising them my benefits were due to run out shortly, therefore no more funds for tuition. The payments provided coverage for only sixteen months of tuition not the eighteen months we expected, creating a shortfall of two months. Helena, acting as the schools superintendent took the initiative and had already contacted the government agency responsible for grants. She already advised them of my unfortunate situation. There was a solution but only if I met and followed the criteria. I promised to answer truthfully the following questions:

Could I pay my own tuition? NO!

Did my family have the means to pay? NO!

Was I willing to work a few hours a week to pay for any extras I needed? YES!

The final answer had to be filled in by Helena.

Would my grades be good enough to continue school and achieve still high marks? Absolutely! The government required a signed document from the school, my mother and my boss to verify my statements. Finally, I would be required sign a contract with them stating I promised to work for three years after graduation so the government could recoup their money through my taxes. YES! YES! And YES.

Unlike the unemployment insurance benefits the school received, this grant also included funds for food, rent, necessities, basic transportation and all the new equipment required to write my government exam. As I signed the legal papers, there were no words to express my relief and gratitude, no longer, having solely to depend on working evenings and weekends to pay for food or rent. The opportunities to succeed were now entirely up to me and I liked the feeling. My humble poem to thank Helena dwarfed by comparison to what she had done for me. Her acceptance by displaying that poem made me proud.

Our last semester went by lightening fast, even though the classes were so much harder. I was now in the coveted senior

71

class, there was so much to do and our weekends would now, be completely occupied with studies. We were the class the other students looked up to and envied. It was our turn to strut our stuff and poke fun at the newbie. We were cool!

Now that I was able to cut my hours at Bob's, only working Saturdays made it easier to concentrate on the importance of graduating. Bob's shop was up for sale and he planned to move to Winnipeg within few months so that worked out positive for both of us. I would be graduating soon and when I was looking for a job it sadly would not be at Bob's. I had learned so much from him and his customers. Bob said getting to know me made him a more caring and thoughtful person.

I was living my dream; finally, I was working on paying customers. As senior students, we each had the ability to build up a regular clientele. We could now accept tips from our customers which was paid to us above and beyond the price of the services rendered and that we were allowed to keep. Our goal now was to take full responsibility for our own work instead of running to our teachers. We had to solve the problems we created all by ourselves. The expertise of our teachers and the support of their knowledge would still be available to us but at this point, we were not dependent on them. Throwing us to the wolves was what our teacher used to say.

We had now earned respect from our junior and intermediate classmates. Without a second thought, we took the initiative and helped our teachers as often as possible. The foremost obsession on all our minds right now other than graduation was landing a job. What good was the education if you had no place to work? Our school was one of the few that promised to help their graduates find jobs -although it was not a guaranteed. With my upcoming marriage to Ron in our very near future, the job I was going to look for with out a doubt needed to be long term and well paying.

I yearned to go back to work for Betty after graduation but sadly that was no longer viable as she had a heart attack and closed her shop. Billie moved to Toronto to work in theatre as a makeup artist and hairdresser, he would be able to use his love of styling long hair to its fullest in this venue. I missed them both very much.

Chapter Thirteen

Everyone in our class was so excited, just a couple more weeks and we would write our government exam. Now was the time for us to reflect on the last seventeen and a half months, a time when none of us knew how to cut hair with a straight razor, do a full body massage, wax someone's face or apply makeup for the theatre. We now each had a clientele, and some of these customers would even follow us to the salons we would be working at after graduation. Most of us had a specialty that we would implement when we started our new jobs. These last days concluded our final challenges as students of Saul Popes School Of Hairdressing. We were outrageously busy, only soon to have it all come to an abrupt end.

We as students shared stories of the weird and wonderful things or people that passed through our lives in our short time together. I remembered fondly, the young girl who came in with her mom and who needed to be taken to the washroom; so I offered to take her. To my surprise and distress, I found her bottom covered with a very thick layer of black hair. I was not sure how to react to this shocking sight but staying calm making sure this little girl did not know it upset me was the correct thing to do. I did wonder however, why the mother did not tell me first or take her herself.

We reminisced about the customer who needed a manicure, her nails all twisted like corkscrews around the tips of her callused fingers. How she would not allow them to be cut only cleaned and polished. It was extremely difficult removing the old polish from the twisted grotesque looking nails. The one service I really detested performing was pedicures; working on people's feet was not enjoyable. Perhaps because they were coming to a school, I felt that some of the customers did not think it was necessary to clean their feet first, and that disgusted me. For that reason, I would not pursue this as part of my career.

The strangest part of the day was yet to come; our senior teacher Mrs. Burns entered our classroom closing the door behind her announcing that this was the part of the course that students were forbidden to talk about. She swore us all to secrecy saying we would spoil it for the future classes if we told. Then in front of each of us on the table, she placed a long thin piece of broken glass. On one side was white medical tape, the other side was a very sharp thin edge. She pointed to the taped side; we were informed that this was what we were to hold onto, as not to cut ourselves. The other edge was for performing a haircut. A HAIRCUT ??? Whose crazy idea was this? Mrs. Burns laughed and said, "We are just getting started." The mixture of fear and excitement could have be seen on everyone's face. I inquired as to who would be crazy enough to volunteer for this class? She just smiled and said, "Pair up all you crazies." Thinking of it today makes me smile.

A Hairdresser's Diary

Mrs. Burns said, "When you leave our school you will be the best and in order to be the best I will require you to do a few apparently ridiculous things." She added, "If you can cut hair with this sharp glass you will be able to cut hair like no one else, so let's begin." To our surprise, we all did much better than we thought we would. To this day, I have yet to have found a reason to use this technique; this probably goes for the rest of the class as well. Fifty years of hairdressing and no one has requested a haircut by sharp glass as of yet, go figure.

Our next obstacle was to wrap a perm (no solution involved just water), do a hand and arm massage, facial and a shampoo, while being blindfolded. Thank goodness, there were no sharp objects involved. Some of us would have certainly failed. None of us could figure out what the blindfolds were about until half way through our task we removed them there were no lights on. "Now" said Mrs. Burns "you will know how to keep your cool and make your customer comfortable if the hydro goes out. " "Keeping your customer comfortable at all times is part of your job." I am 66 now and never yet have I had to do hair in the dark. Was this Frivolous training or a confidence builder? As this day progressed, things grew stranger and stranger. We noticed several people who were not customers walking around assessing our work with extreme interest. Our class discussed amongst ourselves the creepiness of the situation. Mentioning our suspicions to our teachers, she begged our patience just a little longer. The excitement caused a lot of speculation concluding the visitors must be government inspectors. Our teachers would not confirm or deny our suspicions but with our exam coming up that seemed the most likely explanation. To set our minds at ease Helena said, "Pleasant surprises are in store for you all on the last day of school, be patient for now."

With only three days left, we needed to make sure we had everything together, prepping our models, replacing blades in our straight razor, new shoes and uniforms, sterilized and cleaned tools ready. While changing the razors blade I neglected to follow the most important safety rule of holding a towel over top of the blade pulling the razor across a flat surface letting the blade fall out without incident. Instead I foolishly and carelessly held the razor straight up on the edge of my table as the blade came loose it fell back slicing the back of my hand wide open. I was bleeding profusely; I wrapped my hand in a towel and ran the block it took to get to my doctor's Office. Five stitches later and very shaken my worry was solely relating to my exam, if postponed I might have to wait at least six more months to try again. I knew for a fact working as a beautician without that certificate or at least the confirmation it achieved was not possible or legal. My teacher's advice was invaluable. After getting the lecture I wholly deserved she told me to get ready for the exam anyway and just show the examiners the stitches. It was not unheard of that a student might use an injury to get sympathy points. It was important for the examiners to literally, see the stitches before allowing me to take the exam. Imagine how ridiculous I felt for being so reckless, and careless. My stupidity did not warrant special treatment.

You could hardly hear yourself think, for all of the buzzing and commotion in our classroom. In just three short hours, we would be working in front of the government examiners, each with our models - I broke down and asked my mother to be my model. I wanted her to see first hand, what this daughter of hers had learned over the past eighteen months and how good I was at what I had did learn. Helena was pleased with my choice and commended me on having the maturity to ask her. I was pleasingly surprised when my mother accepted so readily, almost with a hint of gratitude. Everything was now in place and was geared up ready to take my exam, stitches and all.

As our class gathered our items together, we saw on our stations a folder. In that folder was a list of names and business cards plus references from our teachers. It turned out the people watching us all last week were prospective employers. Now, we knew why the close scrutinizing by the visitors to our school, who we thought were acting so very strange. My file consisted of seven definite job proposals, three interview appointments and eight business cards from salons looking for full time beauticians. I was shocked, delighted and proud to know my file held the most requests for positions. The next highest was five proposals. It was explained to me, it was my love for and specialty in styling long hair. It was noted that I was courteous and as one employer described me a 'ball of fire'. Dorothy had removed her name from any interview lists as she was going to open a shop in her home and at most would employ one other person. This fulfilled her dream. Saul had accepted a job in St Thomas with a former student, whose shop only employed male hairdressers. The rest of us would choose jobs from our lists of prospects. No one from this class had an empty folder. We were encouraged by Helena, to pass on to others the prospects we would not be perusing, thus giving everyone a better chance to find a good job.

We did not have time to spend looking over our offers as time was running out and we would be late for our exam. I had to show the Government supervisor my stitches and it was explained to me that no exceptions would be made; I understood and continued with the practical part of the exam. This is the portion of the exam where we worked on our models, performing a haircut, perm wrap, head massage, manicure and pedicure. My hand was very painful when I had to put any pressure on it, but I didn't even wince. This was my own doing and I would not let my carelessness make a difference. The theory portion was all written and as it was my right hand I had to write with a lighter touch than usual but readable, none the less.

We had to wait two to three months to get our results. I knew I passed but I was concerned because of my sore hand I might have lost valuable marks. Those that did not pass received notification immediately. They could then choose if they wanted to go back to school for another six months or not to continue as a stylist but to go onto something else.

Chapter Fourteen

The day I had looked forward to for so very long was finally over, and now there was time to look in my folder. I could not believe some of the salons that wanted me to work for them. The city of London had an abundance of high-class shops. I needed to make a decision and soon, I read and reread the letters from the interested salon owners. While examining each's reason for wanting to hire me, I realized several made reference to my specializing in long hair. At that moment, pride filled my heart. Now would be the time to make all those who helped me along the way proud, and the time for me to say thank you, by making the perfect choice. I chose to work for Simpson Sears Department Store for The Elizabeth Arden's Salon. This was the perfect choice, as I had already worked with them through Meg when I was modeling for her. That same week my final cheque came from the government completing my grant I immediately called to inform them I was finished school and working and wanted to know how to get the cheque back to them. To my surprise and delight, they suggested that I keep it. The worker said she could see on my application my nineteenth birthday was coming up and she suggested I should use it to celebrate that birthday. She said," The paper work to return it to us would be more work than the money is worth." I was grateful and graciously thanked her. Ron and I used the money for necessities for our wedding.

Now three days had passed and the rush was over. Finally, I had an opportunity to contact my mom. I wanted to know if she enjoyed the time spent with me and if she liked being my model. I desperately looked for some morsel of praise from her. I asked what her impression of my new career was now. The next few seconds of total silence seemed like an eternity. She finally answered me. "Well," she said, "I did not expect to be left alone with strangers while you finished your exam, you could have at least made sure I was taken care of first."

I tried to explain that the teachers were supposed to take care of our models needs. As students, we were not permitted to leave the exam room until the tests for both physical and written were finished. The penalty for leaving would be a failing mark. I said, "Mom, we discussed the rules and arrangements before you agreed to be my model, I had no idea you had a problem with the plans."

She curtly stated. "Well I certainly didn't expect to have my hair cut, nor did I agree to have pin curls and a finger waves, I didn't like the results. My hair was too flat."

Now flustered, I answered. "But mom, that is what my exam was all about it wasn't a beauty contest." I knew if I was going to end this conversation with any maturity or civility at all, I needed to change the subject. Therefore, I decided to share with her the good news regarding the government cheque that would allow Ron and I to help with our wedding expenses.

With the words barely out of my mouth, she said, "Good then you can pay me back for the ingredients I bought to make your wedding cake." To say the least I was utterly and totally stunned. Now the silence was on my side of the conversation. The understanding between my mother and I was that the cake would be a wedding gift from her and my stepfather. I was so disappointed and deeply hurt I could not even share with her the excitement of my new job.

After a lengthily and painful discussion, Ron and I decided I would accept his sisters offer of her wedding dress for me to wear. The Sunshine's ladies group I sang for, graciously offered to host our small wedding reception. This was in recompense for my singing at their annual celebrations. Ron and I politely and gratefully accepted their offer. Our wedding, which was to be held in our small town, would be the last effort on my part to reinstate ties with my mother. The next step would have to be hers. Bashing my head against a brick wall was only hurting me. From now on, I would share my dreams, accomplishments and exciting days with Ron. He believed in me and loved me with no strings attached. All of this drama was hard for Ron to understand, his family was the total opposite of mine. All he knew was that I was being hurt and he was going to be my protector.

I had one last chance to talk to Helena before I started my new job; she was utterly and completely thrilled that I had made the choice I had. She said in a half whisper, "You have made us all here at Saul Popes very proud and someday, my sweet one, she, will be proud too."

Nodding through tears I answered, "I know she will, but will it be too late for me to care?"

Softly she replied, "It is never too late my dear." I hugged her with such ferocity, as if I was afraid that letting go would make my world become unglued. She smiled as if she knew my thoughts, patted me on the cheek and with that, she wished me well and we said our tearful goodbyes.

Chapter Fifteen

There wasn't anything which could have prepared me for my first day at work. It was wonderful. Everyone at Simpson Sears welcomed me as if part of a big family; some of the people recognized me from my previous photo shoots in the store. For a large salon like this, I expected everyone to be more business oriented, not so warm, and friendly. The store emitted a sense of wealth and high class. This was not a place to shop if you were pinching pennies. The floor space was meticulous, roomy and inviting. The lighting would dazzle you with its crystals dangling from the chandelier like fixtures. Elizabeth Arden clientele mainly used one of the two escalators to the second floor. There was no doorway leading you into the salon, once the escalator reached the top, you were already there. Your next few steps would take you through the famous RED DOORS, the signature of Elizabeth Arden. Susan or one of two other professionally dressed, polite, soft-spoken secretaries at the front desk greeted the customers. They wore outfits that complimented the red - highly glossed decor. The first visible counter was decorated with the Elizabeth Arden cosmetics line, skin care, fragrances, spa products and nail care. Embossed on the front of the counter was their logo. As I entered the salon a little farther, black leather chairs lined up like soldiers, ready to do their daily duty of seating the waiting customers. A few more steps inside and you could see the stylist stations, each placed perfectly between the long floor length windows. Eight in a row but across from them were four more facing the windows making twelve in total. It was obvious; not all the stations were in use at all times. The hairdryer room was separate from the stylist stations but divided only by an arched entrance. Two dryers were designated for customers who wanted manicures and pedicures. Off to the right and behind closed doors was a massage room fully equipped and ready for use. Next to that was a private room, fully equipped for use by a single stylist. In addition, off to the left was a very large lounge equipped with tea, coffee and cookies for customers and stylist alike. My head whirled, as I tried to take in all of the wonder and beauty. Should I pinch myself, douse myself in cold water, or stay in this dream? I was positive my mother, would be proud if she knew I was working here. She occasionally shopped from their catalogue and drooled over the hundreds of items for sale. Everyone knew about and loved Simpson Sears and Elizabeth Arden's. Now I was to be part of it all.

On my initial meeting, Susan, the manager, presented me with a list of duties I might like to engage in for my first three months. There would be a three-month trial period. The time would be used to teach me about the customers, atmosphere and rules. Yes, there were rules. The next three months would determine if Simpson's and I were compatible. They did not offer any services to customers that I had not practiced during my training. I requested to do some of everything, including manicuring and pedicures (although still not happy working on peoples feet.) In addition, I would be a full body masseuse, in their highly, expensive, fully equipped room. Last but not least, I had my own designated stylist station, all prepped with the necessities to get me working immediately. The only item we as hairdressers supplied for ourselves were our scissors, they were sacred to us and NO ONE ever touched them. There is a valid reason for that rule. We each cut differently, some left handed others right handed but at different angles. It is almost like a fingerprint, no two alike. Our scissors are extremely sharp and if we are the only ones to use them the chances of having to have them sharpened is less likely. However, if someone else uses them, their angle of cutting will dull them making it essential to have them sharpened. I found in my long career once you have to have them sharpened they never cut the same again. The other golden rule is never under any circumstances, cut anything but hair with them.

My third day at work brought with it a surprising challenge. I was requested to do my first full body massage, I was a little apprehensive but didn't waver as I had done many at school. Being so tiny, I had to climb almost up on top of my very large customer to reach across her. She took up the entire massage bed and she hung a bit over the sides. The image that filled my mind at that moment was of me slapping her on the bottom of her feet and her fat rippling all the way up to her head and back on its own giving her a self-massage. I found this disturbing and exceptionally funny. As I poured the warm oil onto her back and started the massage, my hands and wrists disappeared into her soft flesh. After that one unsettling event, I chose to use my massage skills for my friends and family only. Employees at Elizabeth Arden's worked together like a well run engine. The pay was better than what I was initially offered and the tips were generous.

One day my boss Susan showed me a letter she received from Meg Daniels. Meg knew I chose Simpsons to work for, so she sent them a copy of my modeling certificate with a glowing reference. Seeing that I no longer modeled for Meg, Simpson wanted me to model for them exclusively. This meant I could not accept any other paying modeling jobs outside of Simpson for as long as I was on their payroll. I was not aware of it at the time, but hairdressing, makeup artistry, and any other related services plus modeling for them was part of my contract. I would not receive anything above my basic pay for any extra work I did for them. Nash Jeweller's an exclusive, luxurious, high-end jewellery store in London paid them handsomely for a photo shoot I did for their Diamond Collection but I only received my regular pay. This shoot was a big deal there were armed guards at my side at all times. That day was one that left me quite unsettled. When I needed to use the restroom, they removed the jewellery and placed it in a locked safe until, I was ready to wear it again. Don't get me wrong I loved modeling and some of the items I modeled were to die for but the work was after hours and many times out of town.

When working with the public there is always the customer who can not be satisfied no matter what and there were a couple of those the first few weeks on the job. Being on probation, I was afraid to mess up. I could probably have handled the problems with a little more maturity if, I was more than eighteen and not just out of school. The first was the cranky pushy customer who was getting a pedicure but wanted me to wax her legs for free. I tried telling her there was a charge, and I did not have the authority to over-ride it. She wanted me to do it anyway, and keep quiet about it. She was very unhappy and embarrassed that I spoke to my boss about it. We lost the customer. I was taught in school that the customer was always right but in this case, I did not believe it to be so. Susan advised me that I should have spoken with her first then maybe, she would have permitted the service and we could have saved a customer. I apologized and assured her, I would not make rash decisions without asking again. My second mistake was the time a customer brought in her eight-year-old daughter to get her bangs cut. Her mother's instructions were "no shorter than to the top of her eyebrows." After I cut them, I checked and they still seemed to be a little too long so I snipped a bit more off, I did this about three more times. Each time her mother sternly reminded me, "Just to the top of her eyebrows." To my and the customers surprise when I was finished, her daughters bangs were too short. I was not able to figure out how this could have possibly happened. I felt awful and the customer was not pleased either. I apologized repeatedly and of course, there was no charge for the haircut. This was policy no permission was needed. The saying from school about the difference between a good and bad haircut would not work here. What was it with bangs? First, mine now a customer's. I knew I deserved the tongue-lashing I was about to receive. Instead, Susan started to laugh. She had run into this problem before, the customers little girl had a habit of raising her eyebrows as she was getting her haircut. Therefore, her eyebrows were always touching her newly cut bangs. "Did you give her the haircut for free?" Susan asked. "Yes of course" I answered cautiously. "Well Chris you will have to pay for it, then that way next time you will pay attention." She added, "A cheap lesson for you." I am not exactly sure if this was fair but a valuable, not cheap lesson anyway.

Not every day was filled with wonder and excitement, we had our routines like anyone else. Every morning our salon opened an hour and a half before the store. That was so that the managers of each department could come and get a comb out; their makeup freshened and ready for the day. Simpson's was very strict about how their managers and staff looked, therefore they supplied the means to insure the results they wanted. There was no charge to the managers for this service, as it was mandatory to look your best. If you could not do it yourself, we did it for you. We beauticians also used the slower times to have our own nails and hair done.

Chapter Sixteen

Patiently waiting for my results and license to come in the mail was well worth it. What a great and exciting birthday present, receiving my marks on my nineteenth birthday and just a week before my wedding. I passed with first class honours, ninety-eight percent in theory and ninety-four percent in practical. The letter from the government stated that I would have had ninety-nine percent in practical, if not for the stitches; that hindered the pressure needed for one of the sessions. I was ecstatic, Ron and Helena were very proud of me. Sharing this accomplishment with Betty would have made this moment even more special. A painful piercing sadness engulfed me. The urge to let my mother know was fleeting. I desperately wanted to shake her up to make her realize what my accomplishments were, so I decided to be safe and send her a letter. In this very long detailed letter, I gave it my all I shared my disappointments and my heartache. I steered clear of any subject that did not relate to my schooling and hairdressing. I was a coward and was afraid to go to that dark part of my life. I told her about my new job and my spectacular marks. I mentioned Betty and Helena, Ron and his family. I wrote about, our upcoming wedding and how I was looking forwards to being married at home in our small town church. I poured my heart out to her for the very first time since I had been away from home. I had always held these painful feeling in as if I needed to protect myself from them. I felt so much better and it felt like a ton had been lifted from me. Ron felt I was wasting my time and breath but I needed to do this even if it was for nothing. We both knew the next time I would be going home would be two days before our wedding and that would not be the time to talk about this. With my heart in my throat, I put the letter in the mailbox. As I closed the slot, I felt a little uneasy. I ran the words through my head once more knowing it was too late to take them back the slot had already closed.

Thursday was a very busy and long day at the Salon as we had extended hours but my day didn't start until noon. I arrived a few minutes early, and Susan was waiting for me. She seemed very excited and overly eager for me to talk to her. She had just received a letter from the head office. They wanted our store to do a TV special, with me as their model. The TV special would showcase a visiting hairdresser from Europe and the subject of the show was something new called "Colours." This new concept was about harmonizing hair colour with skin colour and with clothing. This new technique was about making sure clients had the means to look their best. This was something new to North America; Europe had been using it for years. Each person's skin tone was divided into one of the four 'seasons' summer, winter, spring and fall. Unknowingly we as beauticians had been already doing a form of this when we coloured customers hair. Matching warm skin colour with warm hair colour or cool with cool was something we had done without thinking it was automatic. This new system would guarantee that customers would have the tools to look fresher and younger.

The second reason for Stephan's visit was to introduce us and the TV audience to new kinds of hairpieces. The line would also include partial human hair wigs developed in Europe. This was something new that Elizabeth Aden was interested in supplying to their customers. Stephan asked for me personally after he had seen my picture in the catalogue. Therefore, instead of Simpson's sending me there to him, he decided to come to London. Susan was ecstatic that her store was the one chosen for this great privilege and that I was preferred to be the model. We only had two weeks to get ready, and I was on cloud nine. We had to have the dress department choose and resize a dress for me; the jewelry department had to put together a complete set that would match my dress. Maria our makeup artist was chosen to do my makeup and manicure. I felt the pressure and the butterflies in my stomach fluttered uncontrollably. Needing reassurance I called Meg she was so happy and said, "Don't you worry my dear, you will be great." Adding, "The other girls and I will be watching." Now I was really nervous. For the first time I realized it was not just a few photographers, or other models that would be viewing me, it was the whole city. Yikes!

Everyone had information on what TV station we were going to be seen on. The salon had a TV tuned in at the store as well. Each of us in our own way was excited. The whole show was shot right in our salon. The filming was on a Saturday so Ron would be there to watch as well. Even my family and friends at home would be able to watch me. Ron informed my family ahead of time so there could be no misunderstanding about the time, date or channel. Ron said he received a positive reception from my mother about my exciting news.

I was already so excited about the whole ordeal, that the next pleasant surprise took my breath away and brought tears to my eyes. I could not believe it when Billie walked in the door with Stephan! Billie met Stephan in Toronto at the theatre that he was working at. He knew the TV show was to be shot in London and he knew I was the model. So with that information at hand he volunteered to be the hairdresser for the show. He wanted it to be a surprise for me. After crying and hugging, we had to get busy, as the starting time was nearing .

Like a little girl in a candy shop my heart was pounding. Modeling in front of a TV crew and TV cameras was very different from just cameras or being on a runway. I was used to people watching me during a session but not wide spread like this.

First was the colour theory segment of the show and it was determined I was a basic winter with 'all season overtones.' In layman's terms; I was suited to the deep reds, white, fuchsia, purples, all the cool rich colours of winter, but at times I could wear peaches, creams, and other warm colours as well.

I was comfortable having Billie work on me but could feel a slight shaking in his touch. The hairpiece that made my shoulder length hair look longer, was styled in an up do. WOW! I even looked older. Stephan wanted to show the audience how easy it was to put on and take off this wonderful hairpiece. Coming up behind me, he took the hairpiece between his first finger and thumb and pulled straight up but it did not come readily, so he yanked on it. That finally did the trick, but with it came some of my own hair. OUCH!! He was not aware, that Billie had secured the piece by crossing the bobby pins. This was how we were taught in school making it so the false hairpiece would never move. You would have been proud of me, I didn't even flinch on the outside but inside I was screaming. Both Billie and Stephan were apologetic but my head was exceptionally sore. The realization there were some not so glamorous sides to modeling was acknowledged. Stephan spent the next week teaching us colour theory, coordinating hair, skin, makeup and clothing. We were the only salon in London professionally trained to do this at the time. It was not too long after that clothing stores followed adding color theory to their business.

The departure of Stephan's and Billie's left me a little melancholy. I was going to miss them. Stephan had made me feel important. My confidence was at a higher level now. They both were off to their regular lives. Billie back to Toronto to teach others what Stephan taught him and Stephan back to Europe. Before Billie left, he asked me to be his model in the next international hair show in Toronto. I was already modeling for Victor our champion stylist so with sadness I declined. It was almost impossible to be ready without many months of intense practicing. The fact we could have lunch together at the show in four months was enough to sustain us.

The Hair Show was a weekend of glamour, learning, new products, visiting hairstylists in from all over the world and champions from Canada and the USA. Wild, exotic, over the top hairstyles, vivid crazy colours and embellishments were featured. Everyone that was anyone would be at the Toronto International Hair Show. Stylists who trained under Vidal Sassoon would be demonstrating new cuts and styles. It was exciting for us as hairdressers coming into a new era and being taught a new Vidal technique of cutting hair as well as his new world renowned wash and wear looks. We liked the new looks and the precision cutting techniques he was teaching were all new and exciting to us. Most out-of-towners stayed at the Royal York Hotel where the show was held. This, was to be my first show, I could hardly wait. But the show was later, for now, I had to get my head out of the clouds and back to reality.

Well not totally, I could still enjoy the attention and savour the special moments of the last few days my TV experience and the week spent with Stephan and Billie. Susan was thrilled with the outcome. I received a small bonus for my participation and we were already booking appointments in the evenings for customers interested in the new Colour Theory system. For forty dollars the customer received a customized individual analysis of what their skin tone was or what "season" they fell into for hair colour, makeup and clothing. They also received a mini folder with colour swatches of material small enough to carry in their purse so they would always be able to match the proper colours when shopping. Sears took full advantage of this new system handing out coupons for flyers about special offers for those who showed their swatch folder upon checkout. As yet this was not very popular with the male population but it was used in the men's department to co ordinate clothing on display.

Chapter Seventeen

Today was a day, which would be burned into my mind for the rest of my life. It was November 22, 1963, shortly after noon. I arrived at work only to walk into a room of shocked, horrified, and perplexed co-workers who were tearfully shaking their heads in disbelief. The radio announcer was repeating over and over, "Shortly after noon today, President John F. Kennedy was shot as he rode in a motorcade through Dealey Plaza in downtown Dallas, Texas." The sadness, pain and horror of the news filled the hearts of everyone within listening range. You could hear in his voice the announcer choking up as he fought the emotion we were all feeling. No one could talk about how horrific the news was without tearing up. Customers and staff stopped what they were doing to listen to the shocking news. Each of us handled it in our own way. Some of us prayed, some got very quiet and some wept. Nations shared in the painful and shocking news, a broadcast that would haunt us for the rest of our lives. We all needed answers to the deeply disturbing question, "How could this happen?" The whole world would grieve. So many of us had family and friends in the United States, and we were profoundly concerned how this would affect them. In respect for President Kennedy, his family and his country we closed the salon early.

Chapter Eighteen

On Saturdays we held in store demonstrations. The 'Colour Theory' was a sensation. The customer was seated in a straight-backed chair in front of a full-length mirror. We then draped her with an off white, cloth cape, covering her body totally; her hair covered with a turban style wrap, so only her face and neck were bared. At our fingertips were, 12x12 inch, colour swatches in forty-eight different colours, divided into the four seasons. Those swatches separated into two categories, cool and warm. To determine if the customers skin tone fell into the warm or cool group a large swatch of white and one of cream, would be laid over each shoulder and placed just under the chin. The side of the face that looked smoother, younger and healthier determined our conclusion. Just this one-step amazed most customers. Then individual hair swatches, in a variety of colours were placed over the forehead. This was done to determine hair colours that complimented skin tones. After deciding on cool or warm palates, we went on to select a season. Warm colours divided into spring or fall, cool into winter or summer. We found it surprising that most of the clientele fell into either the winter or cool categories.

As in any job there are unhappy or belligerent customers, this business was no different. While Ester analyzed her customer, the woman argued with Ester about what season she was. The analysis definitely put her in the fall category, 'which as you guessed,' are rich warm colours. She desperately wanted to be a winter there was no way of talking her out of it. Ester was desperately trying to explain to this unreasonable person that it didn't matter what her results were, she could wear whatever she wanted. Ester firmly said, "The colours in the fall palate would be the colours that would compliment you the most." She explained, "This is just a guide to make you look your best." Ester, not wanting to make this customer unhappy, recommended a compromise. She suggested they do some pretend shopping in both seasons' colours. Separately each would pick out items and meet at the dressing rooms to compare their choices. Both were amazed at how many of the items were the same or similar in colour. Subconsciously, the customer had picked colours in the fall palette. Although unaware those were the colours she was drawn to the most. She also chose the black and teal that were not in her palate. Ester pointed out how they enhanced the shadows and lines, making them look deeper and her skin drawn. She finally understood. Before Stephan left, he did teach us a few other tips. One important point, as long as the offending colour is not against the face, wear it. Ester knowing this said, "Let's take the black sweater your in love with and put an orange red scarf around the neck." The customer commented," You have made a believer out of me, Ester. I never would have believed there could be such a transformation." Her customer left impressed and happy. She still preferred to be a winter, but was satisfied she could make fall work. Ester became one of our best colour theory specialists, with a faithful following.

Summer and weddings, were two of my favourite times, and when they came hand in hand wonderful things happened. One bride in particular can still bring a tear to my eye. I still remember the sadness and heart wrenching circumstances and the joy I was able to bring her on this one special day. This amazing young girl was Natalie.

She had her back to me, but I could see in her hands a white bridal veil and a picture torn from a magazine. Susan asked. "Chris would you please help Natalie today?" As she did not have a regular beautician she could ask for, Susan selected me. "I would be delighted," I cheerfully answered. As she slowly turned around and looked up to face me, I felt a huge lump in my throat and a burning ache tug at my heart. Under the silk scarf wrapped around her head and face Natalie had deep, widespread, ugly reddish scars all over her face and neck. She had no eyebrows, no lashes and her hairline was receding on the left side and deeply scarred. Her lip on the right side had no lip line just a very thick reddish ugly scar. She looked at me with the most beautiful, big, hazel, sparkling eyes I had ever looked into. Their beauty was hypnotic and at the same time so extremely sad. She said to me, "Two years ago when I was first engaged, to my Mike I was in a fire and had my face, neck and scalp burned." She continued, "I thought my life was over and I was convinced Mike would never look at me again. But he never changed the way he loved me and today he will prove it forever." She added, "In just a few hours we are going to be married." From what she said, I knew It was not to be a big wedding. Close family members and friends would

101

be her only guests; even so, she wanted to wear her white dress with the veil to cover her face.

I asked her, "By chance do you have a picture of yourself from before the accident?" She went to hand me the one out of the magazine I shook my head and said. "No one of you."
"Yes" she said "but it is just a small one." Without hesitation, she took it from her wallet and handed it to me.

I asked her, "will you put yourself in my hands and let me do what ever I want?" She looked at Susan who was smiling and nodding her head yes. I promised her, I would do nothing that would cause her pain or embarrassment. She whispered, "I don't know why I trust you, but I do, yes I will." Both smiling we entered the salon to start. Natalie drawing her scarf a little tighter to her face and her head slightly lowered.

I had an idea but needed support to implement it. I found Susan very supportive and she offered to help any way she could. My first move was to call the school of hairdressing to ask Helena for a favour.

Her answer was, "Definitely yes." In fact she would have one of her students deliver the items I asked for immediately. Before she hung up the phone she said, "By the way Christine, I am very proud of you, you are so thoughtful and please let me know the outcome." I knew now that my plan was going to be successful.

While Natalie was having her manicure and sitting under the dryer, I gathered up everything I needed and put all the items in one of our private lounges. Susan took the items from the student Helena sent and brought them to me. "Do you think this will work?" she asked.

"Definitely!" I replied. She walked away after giving me a quick hug saying, "For someone so young you have a very big heart." I had a catch in my throat when she said that. I only wanted to do for Natalie what I would want someone to do for me.

When Natalie's hair was dry, she followed me into the lounge. On the mirror, I had taped her small picture for me to work from. I then placed her veil carefully on the couch near her and then, I proceeded.

Once again, I asked if she trusted me and she said, "Absolutely." Kiddingly she said, "Make me beautiful like you."

Detecting a catch in her throat, I said, "I will make you more beautiful."

"Not a chance," she said sadly.

"You just wait and see," I replied with a slight nod and a wink. Everything was ready and with Susan's permission, we had total privacy. We chatted like old friends. I started applying the makeup base using the stage makeup borrowed from the school. That was my favour from Helena, the need to borrow their stage makeup kit. I was being careful not to apply the base too thick but applying enough to smooth out the scaring. I worked carefully and as gently as possible. She assured me she felt no discomfort at all. Next, I drew a lip line with a permanent lip liner to make the perfect shape filling it in with a soft, rose pink stain, which would last all day and night. Then I applied eye shadows that made her golden, flecked, hazel eyes glimmer. You couldn't help but be drawn into them. I drew eyebrows were there was none, very feathery and as natural as possible working around the deep scars. As she had no eyelashes, I glued false ones on, thinning them out to match her picture as close as I possibly could. Individual lashes could not be used as she had no natural lashes to adhere them to. On the bottom lids, I drew hairs individually one by one and curved them to look real. I sealed each step with finishing powder. To remove the stage makeup took cleansing cream so this would last until Natalie removed it herself. I used her picture on the mirror as a reference, taking into consideration the picture was taken two years ago, happily the comparison was fairly close.

Now for the final steps. I had the hairpieces by Stephan available to me. One of them was a partial and would make perfect bangs. The hairpiece, made to fill in around ponytails or thinning hair at the back of the head, today would be used to blend with Natalie's own hair to make bangs. Now she would have some fullness to attach her veil to. All the time I was working, we chatted like old friends and not once did she ask what I was doing or if she could see what I was doing. Natalie seemed relaxed and although I am sure she was anxious, she never showed it.

I was almost ready to attach her veil when a soft knock at the door interrupted me. Susan wanted me to know that Natalie's mother was there to pick her up. I requested a few more minutes to finish up before she came in.

"Natalie, I am going to put on your veil and then turn you around to the mirror. Is that okay?" I asked. "Would you like your mom here when I do that?"

Almost in a whisper, "May I see first please?" she asked. She noticed the smile on my face as I nodded my head. Natalie knew that make up was being applied. She was not aware to what extent. When she turned and looked into that mirror she gasped, her eyes widened and she fought hard to hold back the tears. She gently placed her fingers on her face as if she was touching a very delicate rose petal and softly whispered, "I am beautiful, I am beautiful!" She was shaking as she called for her mother who was now walking through the door.

A tear slowly ran down her mothers cheek as Natalie told her, "I cannot cry mom. I want my Mike to see me just like this, crying would ruin everything!" I assured her that stage makeup doesn't cry off easily. She took a deep breath and hugged me so tight I had to fight to breath. Her mother reached over, taking Natalie's picture from the mirror, and thanked me. She gently placed her hands on either side of my face and kissed my forehead. Natalie walked out of the salon wearing her veil, a smile and carrying her scarf. That was a day like no other; I made a difference in someone's life, a real difference, a lasting difference. Susan said, "You should be proud of yourself I am very proud of you." A call to Helena was in order.

A few weeks later Natalie sent me a picture of her and her Mike on their wedding day. She was walking down the aisle and her veil was exactly were I placed it not covering her face. With the picture was a note from Mike thanking me for bringing out Natalie's inner beauty for her to see. "This is what I see every time I look at her," he said. "It was so important for her to have to show our kids someday. Now she says she will no longer look at her scars the same way again. We thank you," Love Natalie and Mike. I was pleased.

I made a promise to Helena to help others and on that day that promise was kept. Nothing in this life can be more satisfying than to do something unselfishly or to give to another.

When the compliments came from the rest of the staff and a few customers, I thanked them all, but I felt I did what

God gave me the talent to do. I did not ask for or expect the pat on the back received. Although I cannot tell a lie, I did enjoy the attention that I got and deserved but I did not let it go to my head. I felt I matured a little more that day.

Chapter Nineteen

February 1st, 1964, 12:00 noon was my special day. Ron and I would marry. I went home on Friday night, our wedding was Saturday, and we both had to be back at work on Monday morning. Ron's father had the guys get together the night before the wedding so Ron could kiss his bachelorhood goodbye. I spent the night with my mother and the girls who were to stand up for me. We had a good time discussing the demise of my freedom. Then just before we went to bed, my mother shocked me by asking, "Chrissy would you do my hair and touch me up with a little blush and lipstick for your wedding?" She added, "I would like to look my best and that can only happen if you do my hair,"

I hugged her and said, "Mom I would love to I was hoping you would ask."

"Well I didn't want to impose on your special day," She said as she hugged me.

I wrapped my arms around her tightly and whispered, "Thank you mom, thank you," This was the first time I had received any support from her. Then she told me that almost everyone in our small town watched me on the TV show and I had been the talk of the town. Telling me her phone was ringing off the hook and when she went to town, everyone stopped to ask her about me. Mom said there were many towns' people who would be going to the church.

She added, "You are almost a celebrity, and I am proud of you." Wow! Where did that come from? I was afraid to ask in case it backfired. I was now in tears. Ron would be flabbergasted he never expected her to come around. I had waited so long to hear this, what a wonderful, welcomed wedding gift. There was so much more to talk about but this was neither the time nor the place and I needed to just cherish this moment.

It was a very small wedding I wore a borrowed wedding dress bridesmaids and ushers wore mismatched outfits. We only had two attendants besides my niece as my flower girl and Ron's brother as our ring bearer. My in laws paid for the bridal flowers. And my mother was right, the church was full of towns people and some friends from school. It was a cold, crisp, sunny winter's day. After the church service, we had our small reception prepared by the women of the town. Our wedding cake sat on the table in front of our head table. It was a group effort, paid for by me, made by my mother, and decorated by a friend of mine. By the time the reception was over it was storming, making the drive hazardous for those traveling any distance. We spent the rest of the weekend in Hamilton, a few hours away, only to return to work in London, Monday morning.

When I returned to work after the weekend, I was a married woman. Just barely nineteen and so much had happened in my life already. If this was a taste of what was in store for me, with my chosen career and my new life with Ron, then I was in for the ride of my life, and the ride would be fantastic. Having someone so special in my life to share it with only made the ride more exciting.

I was able to move out of Aunt J's boarding house to a small place Ron and I would call our own, a tiny bed sitting room, but it was ours. I was pleased when Aunt J said, "I will miss you and I would not be prouder if you were my own daughter." She knew how grateful I was for her many kindnesses. She wished me well, and I left her boarding house for the very last time.

My work mates greeted me Monday morning with hoots, howls, and wedding jokes. On my station were several wedding gifts and a twenty five-dollar gift certificate from the store. Ron and I were delighted, surprised and appreciative.

Chapter Twenty

Having been employed by Simpson's for six months now, it was obvious I would have employment as long as required. I now had a growing and devoted clientele. It was amazing how the bond between hairdresser and clients grew so strong. My expertise with long hair was widely known and clients from other shops would ask for me. Most of these customers remained loyal to their own hairdressers except under special circumstances. When they needed a unique hairstyle for a special occasion, then they came to me. These customers in fact had two regular hairdressers. Most stylists do not like to share their clients but in this case, this system worked. I even received requests from other salons to help with weddings, graduations or photo shoots when long hair was involved. I developed a way to seal the ends of thin braids with scotch tape. These then could be intertwined with the curls. Using scotch tape instead of using elastics bands was a signature of mine. This ensured no stress on the hair, and braids could be easily removed. I also styled the curls so that when the hair was let down, it was soft and smooth, unlike the fuzziness of backcombing. I also introduced hairpieces into the customers' long hair that made them easier to remove. I styled a brides veil directly to the hairpiece and she removed both as one. Some brides even left their veil on the hairpiece for years for display. I did the same for a young girl who wanted to wear a tiara for her prom. Little things like this did not go unnoticed by other hairdressers or salon owners. This also became one of my specialties.

Dorothy was desperate and asked, "Could you please help me Chris, I have a wedding for a dear friend coming up, and there are four long haired clients, you know how long hair puts me in a panic." Jokingly I said, "Dorothy, whatever I can do, I will. We certainly don't want the long haired boogie man to get you." We both laughed. "How could I refuse you?" I replied, "I have two weeks holidays coming up. It will give me the time to help you get prepared."

"Oh hon, I don't want lessons. I would like you to come do their hair!" She sounded panicky.

Calming her I said, "Okay, not to worry, I will change my work schedule and I will be there." The sigh of relief could be heard a mile away. "Oh by the way Dorothy, I want something in return. You have to feed me lunch."

She hesitated before answering, "But I'm a lousy cook."

Knowing this to be true, we both chuckled."Okay, okay could we at least have coffee and cookies?" I asked.

Dorothy assured me light-heartedly, "That I can do without needing to call an ambulance."

Price was a consideration. Many could not afford to come to Elizabeth Arden's. Part of the deal between Dorothy and I was to keep my workplace a secret. She could not afford to lose customer's so we agreed not to tell anyone. I was her assistant for the day. She was embarrassed about her lack of the knowledge or desire to do long hair. As far as we were concerned, this was a one-time favour. She didn't want to disappoint her lifelong friend. It certainly was the least I could do for Dorothy.

More good news came with this day. Billie was coming to town, and this time he was bringing Vito, a stylist from Italy, who was eager to open several salons across Ontario. While he was here, I was to be his model for the hair show in Windsor. I had to get permission from Simpson for this, but as no compensation was involved they didn't have a problem with it. Ron knew how important this was to me so he didn't even hesitate to say "Honey go for it."

Chapter Twenty-One

My hair now was almost half way down my back and Ron was obsessed with it. He would run his hands through it and constantly tell me how beautiful and silky it was. He LOVED long hair and it pleased him that my tresses were that long. Whenever I was modeling, one of the first questions Ron asked was, "Are you cutting your hair?"

I never hesitated, "No honey I am not."

He would just smile and say, "Just asking."

Billie was intrigued when he saw my flowing locks had grown past my waist. He got more excited as creative vision of what he could accomplish at the show whirled around in his head. He asked, "Sweetie is there anything I can or cannot do to your hair for the show?"

My answer was, "Billie my head is yours to do whatever you please with only one exception."

"You don't want it coloured?' He asked.

"No I don't want it cut, this you have to promise me!" I added. "Neither Ron nor I would be very happy if my hair was cut."

"Not a problem, I promise. I would never do that to you anything else?" He asked.

"No I am totally yours." I said with a hug to seal the deal. I was prepared to come home a different colour or even a lot of different colours. Ron would not be a surprised. This competition was not about the glitz, design or embellishments of past shows. The idea was to see what could be achieved in four, one-hour, timed segments to get four dissimilar looks. Ponytails, braids, twists, use of clips, barrettes, fake bangs, and hairpieces were on the agenda. We laughed as I said, "This time Billie lets not cross the bobby pins on the hairpiece my head still remembers."

Once on stage, each stylists had only one model, so anyone wanting to see the demo on long hair was watching Billie. When he was finished with his last style and was brushing my hair out, Vito walked behind me. As he did, he ran his index finger across the back of my hair just above my shoulders. At that point, Billie picked up his scissors and cut my hair off, just at the place Vito ran his finger. There were no mirrors on stage so I could not see what he was about to do. Show or no show I would have stopped him. I was utterly in shock. I held back my tears but hurried off the stage. Billie came running after me and crying I asked, "Why did you do this to me?" As I asked I was grabbing what was left to my hair.

His flimsy excuse was "Sorry but I desperately want this job with Vito and I am willing to do whatever Vito wants to get it."

Hysterically I repeated, "You promised Billie, you promised!"

"I am sorry, but this opportunity means everything to me, I though you of all people would understand." He added, "I thought we were friends the kind of friends that would always be there for each other no matter what?"

"Billie I will never forget what you did for me, but what you have done to me now is unforgivable you made me a promise." Crying I continued, "Do you think your mother would be proud of you right now?"

Billie tried to put his arms around me, but, I felt cold and betrayed. Sorry was not good enough all I could really sense was that to Billie my feelings or his promise to me was meaningless. He pleaded with me to let him at least finish the job of cutting my unevenly chopped hair into a reasonable style. I refused him; he would never touch my hair again.

It was at that moment, I made a vow to NEVER, to cut anyone's hair too short. No one would ever feel like I felt at this moment, violated, betrayed, hurt, and sick to their stomach. No one on the other end of my scissors would ever want to cry. Frantic, I caught the train home that weekend alone. Billie and I parted ways I never wanted to see him again. My ride home was with mixed feelings knowing my friendship with Billie was jeopardized; the lack of respect for me was obvious. Ron would be furious to say the least. Thank goodness, neither my job nor my modeling depended on the length of my hair. The mess Billie left me with had to be fixed by one of the salon hairdressers; they were curious, but respected my desire to not talk about it. That was no help when questioned about the incident by one of the beauty supply sales people. They had heard about the incident from a hairdresser who attended the show. The person telling the story reported hearing Billie trying to explain to a very angry, disenchanted Vito why he no longer had a model for the rest of the show. Vito dismissed Billie refusing to accept his apologies or so the story goes.

Chapter Twenty-Two

I was six months pregnant and not able to continue working at Simpson's. They had a rule about pregnant employees not working in an environment with chemicals and solutions. This was a time when we as beauticians even had to have yearly chest x-rays. It was made clear my job would be held for me. I was still able to service friends and family at home. One of the benefits of hairdressing was the ability to work from home, only a few careers supported this perk.

Ron and I moved to a bigger apartment with two bedrooms and much more space. We had a baby girl to make room for now. Michele our beautiful daughter, our pride and joy was a preemie but healthy. Ron beamed as he shared pictures and stories of his -daddy's little girl- there was no man prouder than he was. We were nineteen, married, parents and on our way to a life of adventure.

Although going back to work right away was not an option, I continued to do hair at home until I was ready. Three months later, I received a call from Mario who had just opened

Mario's Salon. He opened in London and wanted his salon staffed with beauticians that specialized in their field. Mario said he understood my preference was to work only part time, Thursday and Friday nights and Saturdays. This way Ron could be home for our daughter and we would not have to consider a babysitter. I was surprised and delighted. I soon found out that the reference came from Susan, at Elizabeth Arden's Salon. I accepted the interview and started working the following weekend. Susan and I previously spoke about me working part time and she informed me Simpson's didn't hire staff back part time even on a temporary basis. However, she assured me my job would be there for me when I was ready to go back full time. I thanked Susan for the wonderful reference, and I let her know I accepted Mario's offer. We discussed the pay, would be much more than I was getting at Simpson's. She wanted to keep my place with her open until I decided if I was happy working for Mario. I thanked her, letting her know how much I appreciated all her help. She said, "You are missed, you always brought sunshine in when you came to work, but we all have to do what is best for ourselves and our families." She asked me to keep her informed. Within two weeks, I called to let her know, I would be remaining at Mario's on a permanent part time basis. Susan thanked me for calling, and wishing me luck, she once again reminded me I would always be welcomed back to work for her.

Mario's shop was brand spanking new; everything was shiny and whistle clean. It was pleasing to be in a brand new salon, the smell of new leather, new carpet and fresh paint. What it lacked was the personality, warmth, and hominess that came with age, and with the memories of all of those who walked through the doors. That was okay as we would be the first ones who would leave the first impressions.

Mario was very strict in his policies, and had a great number of rules that we had to follow. His rules did not go over very well, especially with the seasoned beauticians who had earned their place in the respected world of hairdressing. We each knew how to make our own decisions, or Mario would not have recruited us, so we felt he was stepping over the line. Punching a time clock was another thorn. He also expected us to pool our tips. That would mean that Rick, who had the largest clientele, and I, who worked only part time, would get equal shares this was definitely unfair to Rick. Some of Mario's rules would be for us, taking a step backwards. Unlike me, with a shorter time under my belt, these people had many years and a full, faithful, clientele. Although I had a faithful following my clientele was not as extensive as theirs. I was the only part timer at Mario's. My expertise with long hair, makeup, plus the knowledge of the Colour Theory System was the basis of my employment. Jeanie was a hair colour expert, Cecile excelled at precision design cutting and Angie, specialized in manicures and acrylic nails. Rick was the oldest and had a very large clientele; Shelly focused on makeup artistry and massage. We where certainly not limited to our specialties, but having experts in each field to draw from had its benefits. There were three girls to shampoo and clean up after each of us. Our jobs were limited to working on customers, no cleaning up was allowed. I offered once to sweep up after Rick who had just finished a haircut and I was reprimanded. Mario scolded and snapped that he was not paying me to clean up. He went on to say, it would not look good, for one of his professionals to be doing clean up work. I did not understand his thinking, at Elizabeth Arden's we all pitched in to help if needed. It was dangerous to leave hair on the floor. It became dangerously slippery when dry so cleaning it up immediately was necessary. To me, offering to help did not seem unreasonable, but it could get me fired.

This marvellous salon had absolutely everything there was a private room for massage, one for colour draping, another for waxing or for those willing to pay for extra privacy.

Each customer was excessively pampered. In a large lounge was a change room with lockers, where each customer changed from their street clothes to a specially made cotton robe. Each was supplied disposable slipperettes, after removing their shoes, all provided by Mario. Coffee, teas, sodas and water were always available and upon occasion, treats, bought from the bakery located on the main floor of the complex. Mario, himself, was not a beautician, but the owner. He took care of the customers, appointments, and all products and purchases needed to run this grandiose salon.

Several meetings were held with disgruntled employees. We wanted Mario's unreasonable rules and regulations changed. Finally, it was a customer that made him take notice of what he was doing. The customer commented on the tension, which she said could be felt when she came for her appointments. He defensively said he would make sure the staff was instructed to straighten up and be professional. She told him it was not the staff, it was him.

The last straw for everyone was when he booked customers for all of us right up to eleven thirty on New Years Eve. We had all started at six in the morning. As beauticians, we always started early and worked late on Christmas and New Years

Eve. Not many stylists that I knew ever had the energy to go out anyway, but our cut off time was usually ten at the latest.

Bad judgment and his insensible attitude was the start of the demise of Mario's. Each one of us started looking for new positions. We would not be out of work for very long if at all. Somehow, Mario could not understand why we were leaving and he wasn't interested in listening to what we had to say. He called us finicky, spoiled, unprofessional and unreasonable. It was only a few days after we all left that his doors closed. He could not get anyone else to work for him. His reputation preceded him. The rumour was he did not want to sell.

How sad that such a beautiful and well-designed salon could be such an unhappy place to be.

Chapter Twenty-Three

As fate would have it I would never have the opportunity to go back to work for Susan either. Ron had accepted a transfer with his job and we would be off to Burlington. I was very lucky in my chosen field because if you are a good hairdresser you can get a job anywhere. You didn't need a resume just a clientele and or some talent. Therefore, within a week I had a job at Carmen's. They were not advertising for help but I saw the shop while I was driving past to the mall and decided to see if they would hire me. I liked the looks of the shop even from the outside. I auditioned for the job by working for a day free, doing haircuts, a perm and a colour. I started the next week. It always impressed Ron that I could find a job so quickly, almost without effort. Sandra, the only female stylist at Carmen's Salon, was going on her honeymoon and they needed someone to fill in for her. Carmen said they where going to make do but he noted that some of her customers did not like men working on them. Many of the older women preferred female hairdressers. They had not gotten used to the fact that men were not just barbers. Over time some of the customers confided in me that they felt violated and embarrassed when a man worked on them. Many said they found it hard to confide in a man about their deepest secrets. It was amazing what clients told us, it was as if there was a special unspoken trust that was protected by a barrier and nothing could penetrate that barrier.

Peter and Carmen were brothers-in –law and they owned Carmen's together. Peter was very tall dark and slim. Carmen was short, paunchy and balding, a real Mutt and Jeff team. Sandy was the only female all the others employees were Italian men. I was in the company of Peter, Carmen, Vito, Enio, Dino, Pietro, and Salvador. Peter, Carmen, Vito and Salvador were all married with children and their wives and children came in often and brought food and treats. Sandy was a newlywed and of course, there was my family. One day when the guys were teaching me to speak Italian, Anna, Peters wife came in and she very abruptly stopped them. She was angry and started scolding them in Italian. They were laughing but looked like kids who were caught doing naughty things. I was not sure what was going on and when she was finished, she told me that they where teaching me swear words. They all could be heard laughing, so Anna again scolded them. I also laughed and told them I would never trust them again that they had to speak English from now on. These men were wonderful with Sandy and I and for the most they were perfect gentlemen. None the less all thought they were Gods gift to women, especially Dino. I had to put him in his place a few times.

I was sure this day I would be fired. Dino made a very crude sexual remark to me, and I slapped his face and he slapped me back. Ron was furious and threatened to beat him to a pulp.

A Hairdresser's Diary

Carmen asked, "Please don't either of you leave until Peter comes in." When Peter arrived, Carmen tried to explain what had happened and how we were asked to wait for him. Peter listened to my side and then Dinos. Everyone knew Dino had a problem working with females and he would often make very rude sex-based comments to and about us. This time I had enough and asked him to stop for the last time. Ignoring him didn't work. he would just keep it up. Peter was furious and insisted that Dino apologize to me or he would be fired. This made Vito angry as he was Dino's uncle and family member. He said, "Family should come first." Peter said, "I am not going to let it go this time; this isn't the first time." Adding, "Dino you will have to apologize before the end of day or you are gone." They were yelling at each other in Italian but the body language said so much. He did finally apologize but the tension was like a tightly wound spring for weeks after that. Gradually we found common ground and stopped hating each other. We were polite for the sake of customers and our other work mates. Ron on the other hand did not let it go so readily. He was polite but kept his distance from Dino. Peter understood and did not push the issue. Ron for my sake kept his cool but said. "I need you to know honey that no one hurts my wife and gets a free pass from me"

These guys knew how to get their female customers to eat out of their hands. They swooned over them and made each and everyone of their customers feel important. It was funny to watch them; sometimes it was almost as if they were courting their customers, attention, attention, attention. These women ate it up like a box of candy. Anna and Maria (Carmen's wife) used to tease the men unmercifully about flirting,-all the way to the bank. In this case, all the stereotypes about Italian men were true.

When Sandra came back from her honeymoon, I was asked to stay on full time. Ron was happy; he liked everyone at the shop. This time when I modeled at the International Hair Show in Toronto, it would be with Peter. Working at Carmen's was so very different from any other shop I had worked at. Anna and Maria were always having dinners for all the staff or bringing in baked goods. They had barbeques in the summer and always had games and toys for the kids, as well as treats and tons of food. Christine was three now and loved going to these affairs. We went bowling every Tuesday night. The best bowlers we were not but we had a lot of fun. Peter and Carmen were family oriented and included all of our family members or spouses in every salon function they had.

A great deal of the clientele of Carmen's were Italian ladies. I remember the day a very sweet little old lady came in to buy a hair brush. On our counter, we had a basket that had brushes in it priced at four dollars. She stood there for about ten minutes going through the basket, thanked us and started to walk out. Sandra stopped her and asked if she found what she was looking for?

She replied, "Yes but I can get it down the street for three dollars and ninety-nine cents." Sandra looking a little confused replied, "But this is only a penny more"

"Yes" she said, "I know, and if you would price your brushes at three ninety-nine you would sell a lot more." Sandra sold her the brush and lowered the price on the sticker. We laughed at how we almost lost a sale for a penny. We also had a customer who had a routine she was willing to pay extra for. I say extra because she tipped everyone who had anything to do with her hairstyle. Penny preferred Vito to wash her hair, Peter to put in the rollers, and me to comb it out. She was willing to wait for each of us to do our thing. We asked Penny why this was important to her? She said "I like the way Vito shampoos and scrubbed my scalp, the shampoo girls are too wishy-washy about it." She added, "I like the way Peter curls my hair as he put the right tension on each curler." So saying, "It feels like a massage, and I preferred you to style it because it stayed in so much longer." You know the old saying the customer is always right.

Gail was another matter; she was overly well endowed and always wore tops that almost covered something. She would bounce in and make sure she visited every one of the guys. Her skirts were far too short and no one taught her how to sit like a lady. You could hear and feel the stampede, as the guys came running up the stairs from the lunchroom in the basement. No one wanted to miss the free show. Gail was the newest addition to the 'men's only club' down town and I guess she was advertising. It was a joke around the shop, that at least the guys here didn't have to pay admission to the show, the show came to them. She was Salvador's customer and refused to have a shampoo cape put over her, she settled for just a towel around her neck. We could see how hard this was on him, especially when he had to brush the fresh cut hair off her bosoms. This was always the longest drawn out hairdo he ever did. Flirtatiously she said, "It has to be perfect Salvador."

We used a crochet hook for pulling the hair through the little itty-bitty holes in the streaking cap; it was as if we were digging for brains. Alternatively, as one lady put it like we were trying to scratch her nose from the inside. If not done correctly it could feel like torture.

We had Baby Jane (an older lady who had emotional problems) who came in once a month to have her hair tinted as black as we could make it. She would then go home and style it herself. She overly applied her makeup and dressed up to look exactly like Betty Davis in 'Whatever Happened To Baby Jane.' Her sister would come into the shop weekly and she would tell us the story about how her sister became so eccentric. When she was younger, she was in a skating accident and was in a coma for almost 6 months. She recovered but somehow became obsessed with the character Baby Jane. Everyone who knew her loved her and understood. One day at the mall, I watched as she entertained some enthusiastic onlookers and played the part as if she were living it. I too then understood what her disability was doing to her. Being entertaining made her happy.

No one ever left Carmen's to go work somewhere else. I worked there the whole year of 1967 and the full time we lived in Burlington. They opened their salon eight years before and the same people where still there. Even when we went to the hair show, we all went as a group. When Peter and I were in competition, all the other employees cheered us on. Peter, like Victor never won first place, but he had numerous certificates on his wall from competing.

Some of the things people confided in us about were not easy to deal with. We were not trained psychologists and we didn't have professional training, but many times we knew someone who could help. As I said, we knew someone from every lifestyle and profession. Still it was hard to see and hear some of the horrendous and painful things people lived through or had to live with. Mrs. V was one of those clients she would come in occasionally. I believed it was not to get her hair done but for some moral support, just someone to talk to. Her husband, when drinking or stressed, would beat her she would try to hide the bruises with pancake makeup. It did not cover very well, so she would come in to me to get her cover up makeup from the beauty supply. I would try to get her to get help. Each time, she told me he would be sorry the next day. I cried for her and the pain and helplessness she endured. I knew what she said was in confidence, so I had to find a way to help without betraying her. We often shared with each other in the shop some of the more serious problems our customers shared with us. I think we would have driven ourselves crazy carrying all these secrets with us if we could not share. I knew one of Peter's customers was a social worker and I needed to find out what to do. I made it my business to talk to her the next time she came in. Peter thought it was a good idea as well. I had to do the hypothetical scenario, as I could not give her particulars. She said she would drop off all the information this customer would need to get help and next time I saw see her I was to give it to her. The decision to get help she said would have to be the customer's ultimately.

The next time Mrs. V came in bruised, I handed her the packet I received from Peter's customer. At first, she was upset with me but I assured her no one knew it was her or her problems. She was afraid to take the information home in case her husband saw it. I suggested we could keep it here and she could read it in the quiet of our massage room. After the second time, she came in and spent her time reading in the massage room, she asked me if I could arrange her hair appointment to coincide with Peter's customer. I said I would ask and see what I could do. I was not at work when the meeting took place. I can only hope that it was something that helped her.

I left Carmen's only after Ron accepted a transfer to Windsor. There was a big party and many tears. I would miss each and every one, unbelievably even Dino. There would never be another Carmen's for me, no matter where I worked.

Chapter Twenty-Four

I went on to Windsor ahead of Ron, to find an apartment and a job. Like I said before, getting a job was fairly easy for me, this time was no different. Within a week, all was arranged. Now all we were waiting for was Ron to finish his last week in Burlington. I was even able to acquire a babysitter, right in our new apartment complex. Finding a doctor in the office right below our apartment was the icing on the cake. One, two, three all was ready to go.

Never having worked in a small salon before, with only two beauticians, I was bored and wanted to find something more exciting and challenging. Silver haired little old ladies, and everyday housewives, were the majority of the clientele of this shop. Haircuts consisted of trimming bangs or a just little off the bottom. Most customers wanted tight perms, pink or purple hair rinses. I was going stir crazy, desperately; I needed to get my hands into long hair or some upscale styles.

Mary knew I was unhappy and told me about a salon downtown that was looking for a beautician. Thank goodness, for the salesman, who kept everyone informed about what was going on in the world of hair, they were the town gossips of beauty. It was through him she heard about the salons need of a hairdresser.

I graciously thanked Mary and moved on. Out of respect for her help, I sent anyone in that area to her for their needs. At the age of twenty-one, I was not ready for the corner store type salon yet. With a whole lifetime of experimenting and creativity yet in me, it would be extinguished if I stayed there.

I was only in Windsor for a month, and already was working in my second job. Downtown with all the businesses, the shop was super busy, and we had a huge walk-in clientele. One of the reasons I was hired, was to help handle the extra walk-ins. This would be the best way for me to build a customer base leading to a stable clientele. It didn't take long for clients to know me and my clientele grew steadily. I was once again in my element, doing what I did best and enjoyed the most. The money was also so much better. Sometimes tips would equal our pay.

Megan, my new boss, was barely over five foot and large in stature. Her makeup was heavy, but perfectly applied, her tinted black hair had the toussled look. Megan's taste in clothing was both expensive and exquisite her personality, warm, friendly and caring. It was obvious her staff loved her. She ran a tight ship in the salon, and although it was fun, we were expected to act professionally at all times.

She was on top of the newest products and gadgets and was interested in adding the Colour Theory System I introduced her to. The high cost was a factor, so she needed to wait a few months. The next six months flew by, and everything was moving along quite nicely. Word of mouth was either our best friend, or our worst enemy, and my customers had been spreading the good word for me. At times being so backed up, I thought catching up would take a miracle, but the customers patiently waited. I loved my job so much, that days when not everything ran as smoothly as we hoped, were rare.

It was strange, but even clients had conflicts with each other. Two regulars, who were real-estate agents, always seemed to be in competition, not only in their jobs but also in our shop. If we had something new and different to offer, they fought over who would be the first to try it. We had little control over the times customers booked their appointments, but somehow, they always seemed to be booked together. Thank goodness, it was with different hairdressers. It could be quite a show at times. When they got too rowdy, Megan would politely but firmly calm things down. At times, it was very amusing and entertaining.

It was amazing how different working downtown was. It was incredible to see how devoted our customers were, not only to us but also to each other. If one client from a local business came to our shop, you could be assured that at least fifty percent of their staff followed. Many business transactions and discussions happened at lunchtime during our services. Although, I didn't understand much about some of the transactions, I found it fascinating just the same.

Then a black cloud fell over us. Each of us felt like our hearts were broken. Megan was diagnosed with cancer and had very little time left to get her affairs in order. One of those affairs that required taking care of, was to sell her shop. She needed the money for her mounting medical expenses. Megan, tearfully and emotionally, shared her plans to close the shop. She then painfully talked about the raging cancer that was destroying her body. As she hugged us, she whispered her regrets through her sobs. We knew this was her way of saying goodbye one last time. After she left, her husband Neil came in to talk to us, we were all crying and in shock. Why didn't we know? What could we do to help? There were no answers.

Neil gave us all letters of recommendation, two weeks notice, and names of salons looking to add to their staff. It was obvious both of them cared about everyone else. Even at a time when they should not be worried about anyone but themselves, they thought of us. We would have two weeks to tell our clients that we would be moving on. One cannot just walk away without letting the customers know our plans. The sadness, concern and helplessness permeated every nook and cranny of Megan's salon. Both client and staff suffered the feeling of loss.

Most clients depend on us and would follow us to the ends of the worlds if need be. Two weeks passed and when we left that last night Neil locked the door and the shop was it was never reopened again. Three months later we all attended Megan's funeral. God be with you Megan. She will be the Angels beautician.

Chapter Twenty-Five

There are not many professions that work quite the same way as ours. Women are very vain but deeply loyal. What is amazing is the way they feel about their hairdresser. It is almost as if we belong to them. Although complimentary, it puts a huge pressure on us. In the next few weeks, ninety-eight percent of my clientele followed me to Nora's salon, located just down the street. Nora had been the owner of her salon for eleven years, employing herself, four other girls, two shampoo girls, and now me. Everyone worked together helping one another, most times without even being asked. It was not beyond us to throw in a batch of towels that needed to be washed, sweep up after each other, or rinse out a perm or a colour if one of us needed the help. Penny worked strictly on commission, so she could get petty, if she didn't get enough of the walk-in clients. Usually the clients were given to whoever was not busy, but she would get miserable if she was not asked first. Nora liked to keep the peace, so we all worked around Penny. I guessed this would be the only downfall of being paid strictly on commission. Although that would not be the case if your clientele was already established.

For some reason, waxing was more popular in this salon than any other salon I had worked at before. On one occasion, a mother brought her seven-year-old daughter, Effie in, the poor dear had an abnormally large amount of hair on her chin. Her doctors suggested waxing. I personally thought it would be too painful for her but her mother wanted me to try. I practiced on a piece of fuzzy cloth, hoping to get my speed up, the faster I pulled off the wax strips the less painful it would be. It did help somewhat. I however suggested electrolysis, a permanent hair removal done by a specialist. Scarring is a possibility with the needles if not done right, and the cost was high, but pulling out the hair does not permanently stop it from growing back, so it has to be done regularly. I felt badly for Effie, who was amazingly brave during each session.

I drew the line when it came to bikini waxing, that I refused to do. There are specialty shops for that kind of work. Eyebrow and leg waxing was the most popular in our shop.

Wearing fake nails were one of the new growing trends that quickly became very popular and a large part of our clientele wanted to try them. They were thick and clumsy, applied with a glue similar to crazy glue, and then cut, filed, shaped and finally polished. It was not rare for me to have a fake nail stuck to one of my own fingers. Once while applying the crazy glue to the nail shell I dropped it, while trying to catch it in mid air I found it stuck some place other than on my customers nail. It was glued to the back of my hand. Another time when my customer moved to scratch her head my hand was in the way. It did look pretty silly but took a few minutes and a lot of acetone to remove it.

Thank goodness, there was a way to fix these mistakes. I would look awkward and strange walking around with fake nails stuck to me everywhere. On the other hand, maybe I would have started a new trend. I enjoyed giving manicures, especially those times when I was able to decorate the nails with mini artwork.

Larry, one of my manicure customers, the president of a large corporation, liked to have his nails look clean and well groomed. He was very embarrassed the last time he came in for services. I, being a professional, made sure that no one else noticed that he could not stand up straight to leave. I pretended not to notice, and suggested he sit a few more minutes to be sure his nails were dry before leaving. I think he was relieved, and by the size of his tip was grateful.

Even though men worked in beauty salons, none came for haircuts or styles, only for manicures. This would soon change. I knew many men who wanted to be pampered the same as women. We were taught how to cut men's hair in school and the male students, fellow stylists and spouses all needed to get their hair cut, but even in their salons it was always after hours.

Judy was the newest addition to our staff and came with a great clientele. She found that working at her family's salon was becoming problematic, and in order to keep peace, she needed to take a position elsewhere. Judy was used to getting her own way ALL the time and expected the rest of us to be there at her beck and call. Like I said before, not one of us minded helping one another, but we were no ones servant. She ordered us around never asking us to help, just told us. I was just returning from lunch and as I was putting my belongings in our lounge, she barked at me, complaining about having to stand in hair cuttings from two haircuts she had just finished. Her customer looked a little uncomfortable about the tone of her voice. I walked to the back room and brought out the broom, as she stepped back for me to sweep, I stepped in closer to her and very quietly whispered, "Say thank you." The next chance I got, I said, "Judy, I will help you anyway I can, but only when your request it is accompanied with a please and thank you" she looked at me glaringly and continued to work without saying anything to me. When she was finished with her customer, she picked up her coat, flinging it angrily over her shoulder and left for the day. I probably did something I should not have had done, but there is a time one has to stand up for themselves. Nora would not have been pleased with Judy's attitude had she been in the shop.

I was a little hesitant about work the next day. I didn't like confrontation. I was always very talkative and happy go lucky so fighting or arguing was not my forte. Judy was already in the shop and doing a perm when I arrived. She did not say hi back to me when I greeted everyone. Later that day, I was sweeping up hair, and noticed Judy needed some swept up as well. I thought I would show her I was still willing to help. When I passed by her with the broom, she didn't look at me, but said in a very quiet, abrupt voice, "Thank you." I smiled and just kept sweeping. Judy and I never did get very close, and she never barked orders at me again. She was never friendly, but she always mouthed please and thank you.

She only stayed at Nora's for a few more months, then decided to open her own salon in one of the large hotels downtown. Through the beauty supply salesmen's grapevine we heard she was doing very well on her own. Some people work better on their own, no matter what profession they are in, and I feel Judy was one of them.

A Hairdresser's Diary

One thing every salon had in common was, this was a place for sharing everything from first dates to divorces. We heard everything there was to hear, no secrets here. We as hairdressers were born psychologists. We heard it all, shared wonderful news, sad news and had our ears burned with gossip. We would be asked to help solve problems from cradle to grave. Sometimes the quiet of a slow day was a welcome relief. It was an honour for us to share the excitement of a wedding, a birth, an engagement, or the meeting of a true love. It was also a great feeling when we could console those who had bad or sad news, and needed someone to share with. There is a bond between hairdresser and client that sometimes can't be fulfilled by a friend. Our profession demanded trust and the promise to keep secrets. I believe a certain percentage of the population come into salons for reasons other than having their hair done. That sometimes was a secondary reason. There were lonely people who had weekly appointments just to meet someone to talk to. Some needed only to be pampered, as they were lonely and had no one else. One of my regular customers always dozed off when I worked on her hair, as she found it so relaxing. It was amazing how much better a woman felt about herself when she left our salon. I will not lead you to believe that everyone was always happy or satisfied every time. I had disappointments and at times made mistakes. I did my best to fix those mistakes when needed.

Not everyone can get along or like each other. Sometimes that was also true of customers and hairdressers. Personalities clash, therefore upon occasion, we directed a customer to one of the other stylists, rather than losing them from the salon. I have never meet a hairdresser that can satisfy every client they ever worked with, including me. With their blessing, I had taken over some of the other staffs longhaired customers. Feeling uncomfortable, or not enjoying styling long hair, some stylists suggested me. When I knew customers who could benefit by having their hair done by one of the other beauticians, I made the suggestion. Most customers preferred one stylist, but didn't mind when one of the others had to fill in. We were a very close-knit group and there was a trust between us.

This was not always the case in other salons. Some beauticians were too protective of their customers, making it so the fill in stylist didn't have access to the important information needed to service that customer, especially when the colour was a special mix. In our salon it was different, the customers colour formula was in a safe place, but could be accessed by us all. If a customer was moving or wanted to go to another salon, we would supply them with the formula card to take with them. As far as we were concerned, this was the property of the customer. I knew of cases that even though the customer was moving to another province, the salon would not provide the customer with this important information. What was the point? The customer was moving out of province anyway. Customer service no matter what should be one of the first things strived for.

Not having to go into work until noon this day, I was met at the door of the shop by two police officers. After showing my identification and answering a few questions, I was informed that the salon had been robbed. Nora was crying and the others very shaken up. A man, posing as a beauty supply salesman had come in and noticing the lull in the day and lack of customers, took out a small knife and tried to rob Nora.

She said, "He was frightened off when the clothes washer in the back room turned on to the rinse cycle." She assumes he thought someone else was in the shop. As frightened as she was, she threw her appointment book at him as he fled out the door. She missed him but said it made her feel better knowing she at least tried. Nothing was taken, Nora never kept anymore than petty cash in the till, but it was unnerving and frightening. Nora decided she would not allow salesmen into her shop again without an appointment. When I looked her way the rest of the day she was next to tears. We suggested she go home, but she tearfully said, "No bastard is going to scare me out of my own shop." Nora didn't want to tell her husband, Robert, he was a worrier. We convinced her to tell him so he wouldn't find out through someone else. Good move on her part. The only thing Robert insisted on, was installing clear glass panels in the front door, thus giving a clear view of anyone at the door. Also unless the door was kept locked, no one could be left alone! He was adamant about this and made sure each and every one of us had a key. Up until now the only people who had keys were Nora, Robert and whoever had the first appointment each day. Nora was so apologetic the next few days, we felt bad about he guilt she was feeling. No matter how much we tried to soothe her we failed.

Chapter Twenty-Six

A variety of customers, from the very young to the very old, tall, short, skinny, fat, rich, poor, in a rainbow of skin colours shared my chair. Customers with very short, thin, straight hair wanted long flowing curls, those with curly hair wanted straight and those with straight wanted curly. I found it humorous that no matter what, they wanted something they did not have or could not have. Not many seemed to be satisfied with the tresses they were born with, but then if they were no one would need us the lowly hairdresser.

Up until now having time or the chance to talk seriously to Nora concerning a place to offer the Colour Theory System had not been available. She was interested, although hesitant, thinking it might be too modern for most of her older customers. Getting her to agree to let me set aside one night a week for a trial bases was a start. The training starter kit was all I needed to begin. The colour swatches were available from a supplier in Toronto. It surprised me there were no suppliers in Windsor yet.

This would be first-rate for us if it worked out. It certainly would bring in new customers; Nora's would be "the" place to be.

Nora decided we would put up a few flyers posted on our walls and see what came of it. Surprised, we had quite a few enquiries. Later that month we set up and started taking bookings. Customers and staff alike found it a fascinating and interesting procedure. Sometimes it sounded like a game show, people throwing out guesses and comments on the outcome. Often we had groups of three to five come in together. There were times we laughed so hard we couldn't concentrate, it was a hoot. Hearing through the salesman grapevine other shops in Windsor were interested in offering similar services. This was excellent, it meant Colours was gaining popularity and Nora was making a name for herself. I was proud to have been the one to bring it to her shop.

We now had competition, other shops in Windsor started offering the service. Soon I was able to train a new girl, Sara. It was quaint to see everyone's little folders of colour, comparing them to purchases or with each other. It was interesting to listen to friends and family guess the season they thought they would be.

Like the customer at Elizabeth Arden's, sometimes a client would argue or disagree with the outcome and insist we were wrong, wanting to stick to the season they wanted to be. Once I asked a customer, "Why would you pay me to tell you what you don't want to hear?" She answered; "I am not satisfied with the season you chose." I. suggested she go for another analysis and have it done at another salon, offering to refund her money, if they found something different. They did not.

A Hairdresser's Diary

It was amazing how many "colour" customers would use those same colours schemes for decorating their homes. We normally are drawn to the colours we like and most often the ones we choose are in our season. What is uncommon is someone who is more than one season but it happens. I am one of those winters that can wear some spring and summer colours. We who can wear more than one season are very lucky. It was not unheard of that a couple who were two different seasons, living in the same house one being cool, one being warm, might disagree on colours for their homes paint colours, furniture and decorations.

One of the larger men's stores on the main street agreed to put up a colour chart for me. This was an aid for their customers to help then pick the right colours for their skin tones. I provided my expertise to the owner and one of the sales persons. Men who enjoyed this service found that wearing the proper colour made their skin look clearer younger and healthier. We did the colour analysis right there in the men's shop using one of their larger dressing rooms. All I needed was a chair, mirror and white light. They had all three. Men did not go to beauty salons at that time so this was a perfect set up.

Sidney at the men's shop complimented me on how I was able to teach him and his staff that colour choice was important to make one look their best. Overall, sixty percent of the men knew what looked best on them, but the other forty percent needed help and this system certainly made a difference. Men started wearing more pastel colours, mainly in shirts.

One of their customers, Richard, a realtor, went from wearing white shirts to off white and from blue suits to dark brown; he couldn't believe the compliments he was getting. He stated before switching from cool to warm colours he had been told he looked tired. One of the side effects of wearing the incorrect seasons is that the colors can make you look tired or drawn, sometimes inciting the comment, "Do you feel okay to day?" He became a believer immediately, and would be working on changing his wardrobe. Jewellery and accessories are not immune from this rule; cool tones should wear silver or white gold, warm tones yellow gold, brass or bronze. Now don't get this whole colour thing wrong. Wear any colour you desire keeping in mind the importance of not wearing the wrong tone right next to the face. Keep this example in mind. If you love black then choose a scarf, dickey or collar in your seasons colour against your face. Enhancing a wardrobe without replacing, it was the lesson. Nora was delighted with our results.

Sara, busier now than ever, had to add more days to her two day a week schedule. Not wanting to continue with the Colour Theory line, I gradually opted out making my focus hair related. Sara designed her own colour packets. These contained of a variety of colours not in the originals purchased from Toronto. She included an extremely extensive detailed list of complimentary colours for face, accessories and hair. She definitely enjoyed this career, it showed in her work. Sara and I in most cases immediately knew what season a customer was without the draping procedure.

Jenny was new in town, she was looking for a new hairdresser and she was a real hairdresser's challenge. She sported pitch-black hair, which was very unbecoming and phoney looking. Her previous hairdresser, reluctant to try something new, stifled her attractiveness. She needed some life and shine in her hair. Natural black hair is either a very, very dark brown, so dark it looks black, or a blue black that has a blue tinge in sunlight. In nature, there is no such colour as just black. The black used to colour Jenny's hair was not acceptable for two reasons it had no shine plus her skin being so pale made her look far too old and drawn.

For three weeks, I tried unsuccessfully to convince Jenny a less harsh colour would enhance her looks but I failed. Finally, I used wigs to demonstrate what the difference in colour could accomplish. Thanks to Nora, having numerous wigs on hand made it convenient to convince Jenny to try something new. Even with the wigs, I was met with resistance. Only after insisting she wear one home was anything accomplished. Gino, her husband, flipped. He said, "You look younger and sexier, I really like the look." Next day we were changing Jenny's colour. She was very particular about her style, which had not changed in years either. Upon occasion she would invite my family for a day in the pool at their home. In exchange I had to do her hair before I left. Gino begged me to spray her hair it so it would not move. Jenny refused to have sex if it meant messing her hair. In my opinion, Jenny's hair looked more or less the same when she came in as it did when she left the shop each week. She shared obsessive rituals, every night before bed wrapping her head in toilet paper holding it in place with medical tape. What an uninviting sight. I am sure hubby was thrilled with the Frankenstein look. Obsession was the only word that came to mind when I thought about Jenny and her locks.

She wore her hair exactly same style always, no changes ever! She teased me saying I could do her hair with my eyes closed so it was in her will that I be the one to do it for her funeral. This way she would not have to sit up and demand changes. Not everyone shared the hilarity of this situation, calling us morbid, ghoulish and blasphemous. Those were just a few of the uncomplimentary remarks. We saw the humour.

Thank goodness not everyone was so fussy. Jenny, Gino, Ron and I became close friends enjoying many common interests and family gatherings.

I missed Marylou, losing touch after she remarried. I didn't know where she was. Jenny couldn't take Marylou's place but we became the best of friends too. We often laughed, finding the humour in the sneaky approach it took to have her hair colour updated, she thanked me a million times.

Just when you think you have heard and seen everything another surprise comes at you. Ann, one of my former clients referred Bridgette to me. While combing her hair she reached for my left hand, tightly grasping it in both of hers and pressing it close to her chest. The harsh unexpected movements made me lose my balance. As she did this she cautiously whispered, "You don't know this but I am a good witch, I know things I want to tell you but you need to give me permission," I must have looked dumbfounded. I felt sceptically uncomfortable; she assured me there was no harm to me and what she had to say would help prepare me for the future. I was not confident I wanted to trust her. Part of me was obviously curious, and part was eerily uneasy. Once again, she made it clear that she could not share her findings unless I gave her permission. Finally, I agreed, she seemed kooky but looked harmless.

Letting go of my hand, she started to speak in a soft whisper as if only I was to hear. "First of all I predicted you will have five children." So far, I only had one but anything was possible. Her next prediction, "You will come into a fair amount of money, but not until you have suffered for it." She also told me, "Nora will be your employer for less than two years." Saying softly," You would be moving on and as you do things would only improve". I listened, but was not sure what to make of it all. When I was finished with her hair, she again took my left hand in hers and with sincerity said, "You will always be blessed with goodness you have a good and understanding heart." She repeatedly insisted, "Write everything I just told you down and put it in a safe place for future reference." I thanked her and she left. I wrote everything in the order she said it, but it left me visually shaken. I was not one to entirely believe in all of this but I was not a non-believer either. I put the paper in my smock pocket. The strange thing is I didn't share this with anyone at the salon and I never saw Bridgette again. Ron just laughed and just shook his head in utter disbelief when I told him.

***

It was not rare for strange, weird or exciting things to occur almost on a daily basis. We had a client who tried to bleach her hair with household bleach badly, burning her scalp, and losing a good portion of her thick, wavy hair.

Another client shaved off her eyebrows and plucked out her eye lashes on advice of her sister in law, who insisted shaved hair grows in thicker. She thought it would work for this too.

How about the lady that butchered her daughter's hair with small pruning sheers while she slept. Her daughter wouldn't sit still when she was awake. When I asked her why she would do such a thing she said she didn't have time to bring her to us. Well she had to make time now. Weird, crazy, overwhelming things like this happened often. There definitely were those lulls when nothing strange happened but that was no fun. We could file hairdresser's stories under the heading Strange But True.

Chapter Twenty-Seven

Nora was exceptionally generous and allowed us to use any salon service available, as long as we paid for products used. This was unlike other salons, that treated us as if we were just another customer. It seemed redundant since we did each other's hair. It was good business for us to be professionally groomed.

One day while having my hair streaked, the bleach had been washed out but the toner had just been applied. It was then that I received an emergency call from the babysitter. My daughter Christine had been rushed to the hospital and I needed to go immediately. Not having time to wash off the colour or take the streaking cap off (until my hair was finished processing) I wrapped my head in a plastic cap. Putting a small bottle of shampoo in my pocket, I then took a cab to the hospital. This outrageous look attracted a lot of unwanted attention, but that was not my concern at the moment. Once Christine was taken care of and out of any danger, I used the tiny bathroom sink in the ladies room to wash the yuckies out of my hair, before my hair became damaged. Unwilling to leave my precious, scared, little girl in the atmosphere of a cold, daunting hospital without me, left me no alternative but to cause embarrassment to myself. The nurses didn't find my sweet one's swollen glands as entertainingly interesting as my hair saga. The next few days at work, I was the brunt of all kinds of jokes. It was all in fun.

My deep-rooted belief was if something disparaging, clumsy or just plain stupid could go wrong, it would, to me. I was used to having uncanny, weird things happening to me. It was awkwardly difficult to walk with one foot in my mouth so often. Nothing was surprising when it came to my clumsiness, awkwardness or silliness.

While at home one day I decided to cut my hair, a common occurrence. With my scissors in hand I was cutting just above my ear. I thought I heard someone at the door. I turned my head to listen closer, realizing it might just be Cercie our cat. I turned my head back, which caused me to stab myself in the side of my head with the tip of my exceptionally sharp scissors. OUCH! Anyone knowing about scalp wounds knows how profusely they bleed. I had blood spurting like a small geyser from the small triangular wound. I felt it run down my ear and neck. Shock and panic set in. Holding my finger on the wound, I ran across the street to my neighbour. Without knocking, I ran into their house. Fiona fainted as soon as she saw the spurting blood. Her husband Dan came in and found her lying on the floor. Trying to calm me and revive his wife, he informed me Fiona fainted at the sight of blood. No kidding! I think I could have figured that out for myself. I apologized and in tears, I ran back home, unsure what to do next. Dan called after me wanting to make sure I was okay. Afraid to remove my finger from the hole, I called my doctor for advice. It was suggested I remove my finger, to check the bleeding. Yes, it had stopped, so I asked about a tetanus shot. Snickering, the nurse said, "I will ask the doctor as soon as he gets up off the floor from laughing!" I admit it was a painfully stupid thing to do. Ron shaking his head in total disbelief, said, "Honey if you want to commit seppuku (Japanese form of suicide via sword) you have to aim lower, a whole lot lower" and then he broke down hysterically laughing. The sore spot on my head was nothing to the unmerciful teasing I received from family, friends and co-workers. Someone walked past me at work and whispered, "Snip, snip," then smiled and winked. One of the other girls yelled across the room, "Anyone got scissors in their head, oh I mean hand," every one would burst out laughing including me.

By the way, my neighbour Fiona was just fine, but she requested I not bleed at her house any more.

Chapter Twenty-Eight

Not in a hurry this day, my first customer was not coming in until ten thirty. After a very insanely busy few days, a lazy day would be gratefully welcome. Shelly was coming in for her regular, monthly eyebrow and chin waxing. As usual, she brought coffee and was prompt.

When Shelly removed her glasses, I noticed a red, scaly rash on her nose. It had spread to her cheeks, so I asked her about it. She stated, "My sensitivity to the plastic on my glasses is causing me a painful case of psoriasis." Nora has carried a wide supply of Aloe skin care and health products at the shop. Therefore, I called the beauty supply, looking for something that would help Shelly. She was delightfully pleased that I would do that. I asked for a senior staff member who might have more information and I started by telling her about Shelly's nasty rash. She requested a detailed description of Shelly's symptoms. Trying to make it easier for her to understand, I said, "The rash is red, scaly and sore looking she says she has syphilis of the nose."

"WHAT!!" exclaimed the saleslady? Perplexed by her reaction, I repeated my statement once more. Shelly was across the room, waving her arms franticly and desperately trying to get my attention. I waved back putting up my index finger asking for one moment as the sales clerk was asking me for information.

She kept interrupting, frantically repeating, "Chris, Chris, hey Chris." Letting her know I was busy talking I waved her off.

The saleslady finally asked, "Do you mean psoriasis?"

I reply, "Yes, isn't that what I said?"

She was laughing so she could hardly speak, saying," NO! You said Syphilis." Oh my goodness! No wonder Shelly was waving her arms at me. Oh no! I could not have said that? Could I? The saleslady still laughing promised she would not share my folly with anyone else. I was so sorry embarrassed and apologized profusely to both the sales lady and Shelly.

Shelly just laughed and asked, "So did they have anything for the syphilis on my nose?" Now forgiven, we both laughed and agreed not to tell anyone else my slip of the tongue. She stated though, "I am glad I don't know the people at the beauty supply."Yes, Shelly did get cream but from the drug store and without me.

My life was full of these (mouth does not work right moments.) It's funny, when you say or do something stupid everyone remembers but when you say or do something smart, no one remembers.

Having had an extremely frustrating drive to work the next day and upon my arrival, Nora asked why I was upset. I told her that some lame brained idiot was driving erotically in front of me and almost hit an elderly lady crossing the road. Nora placed her hand over her mouth, trying to muffle her laughter making comments like, "Were they nude?" or, "Did they have kinky clothes on?" I could not see the humour, and I was annoyed, until she explained that I had just told her about the "erotic" driver. By now, everyone was howling and laughing so hard they could hardly catch their breath. Oh my God! It finally hit me erotic should have been erratic. The appalling images that were running through my head at that moment were repulsively disturbing. The driver of the other car was elderly, and erotic didn't fit the image. Ask me if I lived that faux pas down quickly? Not bloody likely! Oh well, a day with me was at least lively.

Chapter Twenty-Nine

I now had a large, dedicated, happy clientele. Most of the customers who followed me from Megan's, also brought me new clients over the next few months. The colour theory sessions also expanded our clientele. I was busy constantly; my regular customers were booked on a weekly basis, months in advance. No longer did I have time for colour theory, manicures or waxing. Nora insisted on my having my own personal assistant to help with my customers. It is a bona fide accomplishment to have earned this privilege. My assistant was very much like me when I first started; she was in the government apprenticeship program.

There is no easy way to explain to you how much I loved my work. The busier I was the happier I was. Often dragging my tired, achy, exhausted but contented body home, knowing a good night sleep would rejuvenate me. I was in a satisfying, comfortable and stable position as I had been at Nora's for three years now. If truth be told I sadly missed the modeling portion of my life. Working here there was no reason or need for me to be modeling. I taped a few of my extraordinary modeling photos on my mirror, proud of that part of my life.

More blissful news for our family, this time my pregnancy would not see me laid off work. Nora's motherly instinct immediately clicked in. She was concerned about me working too hard. My customers were both excited and delighted for me. At times, I was inundated with a harem of mother hens wanting to touch the belly and take care of me.

Medical complications caused me to take emergency leave from work and I delivered our son prematurely. Ron was now the proud daddy of a handsome, preemie baby boy. Terry was so very tiny and suffered with some medical problems due to his being a seven-month pregnancy. Christine, now five, was excited to be a big sister. We were so pleased and Terry was such a good baby. I didn't want to rush back to work, but financially it was not an option.

I returned to work after three months leave and it was very apparent I was missed. Although my customers had been well taken care of, they came back to me. Everyone likes their tender ego stroked and I am no different. To my pleasant surprise, my station and chair was laden with baby gifts from warm-hearted and generous customers and staff.

The grapevines of the beauty business, where the salesman, from the beauty supply companies, who made calls to the salons on regular bases. Sometimes they seemed like little old ladies spreading gossip and stories from shop to shop. If there was anything of interest concerning any other salon or stylist, they always had the information firsthand. It was through them, that we started to hear so much concerning Joel Wilders hair Studio and the Wilder family. The entire family was prosperous and each owned their own lucrative businesses. Joel had his hair salon; his brother owned a photo studio, his sister a very pricey and exclusive clothing store and his parents a very fancy and expensive restaurant. Joel, the center of conversation, had just been awarded 'Stylist of the Year' by the largest Windsor daily paper. He also received much deserved recognition for working with the cancer society, and for providing human hair wigs for their clients. He was known for collecting human hair from customers, donating it to companies that wove it into wigs. Everyone in the hairdressing community respected him for his charity works.

Joel's salon was smaller than what Nora had but was more specialized and more luxurious. Once becoming a salon owner or manager, invitations to Joel's events were expected and graciously accepted. Nora attended every one she humanly could. He was heard on several occasions to say, "The more involved the community was, the better off the community." Every stylist who had a thriving reputation wanted to work with or for Joel. As a mater of fact, his whole family was thought of in their subsequent fields with the same respect. Jodie was secretary and manager of his salon. When Joel entered the hair shows held in Toronto, Jodie was always his model. She was knock down gorgeous with an abundance of class and a heart of gold. This description was the voice of understatement.

The salesman's grapevine was the umbilical cord to our community, sometimes feeling a bond without ever meeting the subjects of conversation. It was always rewarding to know our profession was not one filled with unsavoury, uncaring people. I was proud of those in the beauty business I had worked and associated with. One would think that with so many salons in

Windsor, there would be a lot of completion for customers, but I never knew that to be the case. Personally or business assassination was not a norm in our field against another beautician or salon. Don't get me wrong there were always those who broke the mould of honesty and indiscretion. Everyone works differently and I'm sure my work was not always praised or appreciated by others, but bad mouthing another's work does not make one more productive. At one time or another, each of us has had to fix another's mistakes. We are only human and mistakes are inevitable. Although some of the work we saw was not only unprofessional but down right criminal, we could only do was our best to repair it. There was one customer who had exceedingly over bleached hair and when wet it looked and felt like cooked spaghetti. She wanted a perm. My refusal to perm her badly damaged hair was not received graciously, even after informing her the hair would melt into a mushy mess, she threatened to go to another salon. Upset with me she stomped out of the salon only to return the next day in an uncontrollable state, showing me between the sobs, pieces of her hair as well as the places on her scalp where hair used to grow. The perm solution melted her hair between the perm rod and the regrowth and fell off, still wrapped on the rods. She wanted to sue the hairdresser for damages. I felt she was almost as much to blame as the incompetent hairdresser. All I could do was try to do what I could to help mend the damages. Part of me felt partially to blame, I should have been more persistent. Nora assured me that nothing I said would have saved this client from sabotaging herself. The customer finally admitted she signed a form releasing the salon of any responsibly. The customer has to take some responsibility for what happens too. Every competent hairdresser was aware of the risk of over processing damaged hair when you apply perm or any other solution on it.

I ended up cutting her hair as short as I could to get rid of all the damage this was the only solution. I think she was lucky she had at least three inches of regrowth to work with. Thank goodness, there was no permanent damage or scarring to her scalp.

Many people expect a lot from us so my favourite saying was, "I am only a beautician not a magician." Books or magazines touting different hairstyles were an irritant to me. Some customers thought these books were gospel, actually asking for styles or cuts they saw in those books. Saying, "I want to look just like this" pointing to a style. For the most, clients neglected to take into consideration the thickness, length or condition of the hair or the shape of the face and head. Sometimes I felt like a smooth talking salesman convincing a client into thinking the changes were their own idea. The art of persuasion became one of my responsibilities. Part of our training focused on us knowing what would be most suitable. Most times, I was right, yep I said most times.

Chapter Thirty

It was Friday, the second Friday of the month and I was waiting for Mrs. Knowels to come in for her regular hair appointment. I was apprehensive, knowing what was in store for me. The same aggravating problem occurred every two weeks no matter what I said to her or her six-year-old Mindy, and the problem continued. I had to speak up for safety sake. Aware I might lose a wonderful and devoted customer caused me to tread with caution. She followed me from the very first salon I ever worked from in Windsor. As beauticians, we depended on customer loyalty just like hers.

Tactful but firm, there has to be a polite and gentle way of getting my point across. No longer was I working in a small, cozy, two-chair salon where space was restricted. Nora's staffed eight beauticians. We had too many chemicals, scissors, hot irons and customers who didn't like nor deserve a precocious child menacingly running around the beauty salon. My main concern was of course Mindy. Doing my job efficiently or safely while watching Mindy was not a viable option. Past experience taught me that once under the dryer, Mrs. Knowles would not be watching her either.

On that morning, once again I tried to tell her how dangerous it was for her to bring Mindy unsupervised. Again, I knew she was not hearing me. Juggling my customers, Mindy and my growing frustration, I knew this time had to be the last. Wracking my brain to come up with a suitable solution without making matters worse was making me feel ill. There was no easy painless way to bring this to an end. While she was preparing to pay, I hesitantly handed her the bill. On the bottom I had added fifteen dollars for babysitting. She snatched the bill from my hand, and without raising her voice demanded an explanation. Hearing the sharpness in her voice made me feel apprehensive about my chosen method. I explained to her in a friendly and concerned voice how worried I was about Mindy being allowed to roam the salon freely. How impossible it was to give her the attention needed to make sure she was safe. I was trying desperately to stress upon her the horrific disfigurement and damage that could be caused by scissors, hot irons, and chemicals. This was not taking into consideration the annoyance or disturbance of customers who came to relax. I also pointed out to her that on many occasions I had expressed my concerns on this important matter. She crumpled the bill, throwing it into the nearby garbage can, storming out and not leaving her usual twenty-five percent tip.

I was now feeling dreadful about the manner used to get my point across. I felt this was the best way for all concerned. Sadness pulled at my soul. The thought of losing a wonderful customer and friend sickened me.

168

A Hairdresser's Diary

Every morning the first thing any of us did was to check our appointments for the week. To my delight Mrs. Knowels had indeed booked her appointment for her usual Friday afternoon. Betting it might be a mistake, I place a question mark beside it, but when Friday came, in strolled Mrs. Knowels ALONE!! Warily approaching me giving me a big bear hug and in an apologetic soft voice she thanked me for caring so much. Wiping a tear from her cheek she explained that because I was always so nice about her bringing Mindy she didn't think I was serious about leaving her home. She said softly, "Mindy really likes you and I didn't stop to think." Sighing, she added "Plus how could I live without my favourite stylist?"

I was pleasantly relieved that all of this was resolved amicably and there were no hard feelings. Yes, she still brought Mindy for her haircuts but on a day that was less rushed, calling first to make sure I was not too busy so we could also visit.

Sometimes being too nice does not accomplish as much as being straightforward. We both learned a valuable lesson that day. There was a sigh of relief from the other staff now that no one had to worry about Mindy and her safety.

Nora complimenting me on the way I handled the situation also pointed out how it could have backfired. We put up a pegboard for the next week listing some dos and don't for us and our customers. The number one item on the list, was the concern of children being left unattended.

Chapter Thirty-One

One of the most frustrating conditions for an older woman was having their hair styled, then having a hot flash. The newly finished hairdo became soaking wet, undoing everything. More than one of our customers had to deal with this frustrating problem. We as beauticians felt bad but all we could do was to restyle it for them. I was far too young to understand what they were going through but I could feel for them. This was not only time consuming but also an embarrassment for many.

One of the things I enjoyed most about my career were all the different people. With a world of diverse backgrounds, I learned so much about other interesting cultures and their immense range of cooking ideas. The fact I loved to cook foods from all around the world this was a definite plus to my career. I had my very own cooking school housed right in my own beauty chair how perfect was that? When my customers brought me homemade foods from their homelands to try, I was honoured. There were some awesome cooks in my clientele.

We had our own yellow page phonebook right at our fingertips. If items could be made, sold, fixed or decorated, we always knew a clients who could achieve that or knew someone else who could. From chef to funeral home owner, banker to bus driver we knew them all. If you stop to think about it, do you know anyone who has not been touched in one way or another by a stylist or barber? The clients that came in for a service could be rubbing shoulders with an elected official or the town gossip and never know the difference.

***

With a faithful following, I was amazed at what they remembered: birthdays, anniversaries, our children's and spouses names. In a way we became part of their extended families.

Valentine's Day, Christmas, St Patrick's Day, and New Years Eve always brought us special gifts or extra generous tips. New Years Eve most of us would make more in tips for that one night then we would make most of the year. Don't get me wrong, we worked hard and long for those tips going non stop all day and evening. On those crazy, hectic days, lunch and breaks were on the run and most times, we were lucky to have enough time for bathroom breaks. If I didn't know better I might think a hairdresser invented DEPENDS. Everyone wanted to be stunningly fancy, and I for one limited my customers to styling only. I did not offer haircuts, perms, colours or any other service on those days. I advised my customers who wanted any extra services to have them done the day or week before. My customers didn't have a problem with this very strict rule. Everyone expected to have their allotted time in the stylist chair and I accommodated them. This was our night to perform miracles. To be honest sometimes I amazed myself.

A Hairdresser's Diary

As explained before a good percent of my customers had long hair so of course it took longer than short hair but I had a perfectly maintained system. Some of these customers had hair half way down their back, which took a very long time to dry, so they came the day before. I would set their hair in rollers and let their hair dry naturally over night. They returned the next day to be styled. This worked very well and no one minded. Funny this was a time when it was not unheard of to see women strolling through the mall, or down the street with rollers in their hair.

I used elastics to divide the hair into three or four separate and strategically placed ponytails. Then I designed cascades of curls, from those ponytails the curls and braids all intertwined into one another. This saved time, back combing and all the excessive pins needed to keep the hair in place. This was easier on the head and when the elastics where cut, and the pins removed, there where no tangled backcombing knots or frizzles to deal with. I was blessed to have a customer base that not only appreciated my unique way they also bragged about my work to others.

It was amazing what we invented to make out jobs more efficient, faster and easier. I used scotch tape for many of my styles. If for instance, a customer required straight bangs. Taping them flat to her forehead while wet, then placing her under the dryer, the hair unable to move, remained straight. Perfect bangs every time. For better hold and body, using a mixture of red jello with hot water made one gallon of the perfect styling gel. I was not sure why this concoction worked but it did. Nora thought I had invented the best thing since sliced cheese, so we successfully used it on a permanent basis. It was every bit as effective and a lot less expensive than the professional setting lotions, and it was alcohol free.

Those few hairdressers who thought hairdressing was just a quick way to make money, never understood how important customers' tresses were to them. This is one of the few professions where creativity, ar,t and trust all go hand in hand. My customers trusted me wholeheartedly, with blind faith to do my utmost to make them look and feel their best. My promise, although unspoken, was that I would do just that. They 'trusted' my opinion on shampoos, conditioners, sprays, colours and other commercial hair products. They 'trusted' that I would listen to them when they had things to share. They 'trusted' that when I touched them it would be in a safe and healthy manner. They 'trusted' me to keep their secrets when they bared their souls. Most doctors don't share such a closeness with their patients. Hairdressers are persons that everyone, at any age, profession, or walk of life benefits from. We need to cherish that safeguarded privilege. This was not something new it is age old. The impact we have, should be taught in beauty schools, as well as how we could use our knowledge for betterment.

I have a disconcerting memory of a customer who cried for a week. She felt ugly after a hairdresser finished giving her a very bad perm. This incident ruined her family pictures, which could never be retaken. In this case, a wig would have been the perfect fix.

That however was not always the case. One important suggestion I had for my customers was NEVER have a colour, perm or hair cut the same week as they were having pictures taken, going out for any special occasion or celebration. There's nothing worse than an unpleasant surprise. Even if you have had the same hairdresser for years unforeseen things can happen. The face is the canvas but hair is the frame. Without the frame, the canvas never looks finished. The frame however can look great without the canvas.

Chapter Thirty-Two

This was a very exciting day for me. I could not believe the way things came about. Just three days ago, I was working for Nora and thoroughly enjoying my job. I had everything I wanted or needed, or so I thought. Nora's was an upscale salon compared to the two small shops I worked in when we first moved to Windsor. I was certain, I would be working there until I retired, or moved again, whichever came first. The last three years went by so fast. Ron and I discussed work everyday but never had we discussed me working somewhere else. Anyone who knew me would tell you I was happy at Nora's. But something very strange happened and everything changed.

I was at lunch just three short days ago, at a small lunch deli, when the waitress, Lora asked, "Are you Chris?"

I answered; "Yes."

"Do you work for Nora?"

"Yes."

She continued, "Are you Chris who specializes in styling long hair?"

I was now very curious. "Why do you ask?"

She added. "I heard that Joel from Wilder Studios was looking for you."

"Me? Are you sure? Why?" Surprised, I asked.

"He needs a long hair specialist and heard about you."

"WOW!" I exclaimed. "What a compliment."

***

Wilder Studios was the most prestigious salon in all of Windsor. There wasn't a hairdresser that wouldn't give almost anything to be working there. Each beautician was in his salon because they specialized in their field. Lora suggested I go pay him a visit. Getting up the courage to talk to Joel, I needed to find out for myself if the rumour Lora heard was true. Expecting Joel to be in a large, fancy, main street location I was surprised to find him located on a side street in a small-unadorned salon. A small sign over the front door said 'Wilder Hair Studios'. As I walked through the recessed, plain, heavy, wooden front door, I could smell the difference in the air. The scent of expensive perms, fragrances hairspray, high priced shampoos and conditioners permeated the air. To the seasoned beautician, there is a difference in the scent of the lesser expensive products versus the higher priced ones. The staff wore no uniforms, just smocks when necessary; all five stylists wore their street clothes, no nametags or nameplates above their mirrors. A warm, friendly, welcoming, yet exclusive atmosphere embraced me as I entered the front door. Wilder Studios exuded class and money.

I informed the secretary, whom I assumed was Jodie, that I was looking into a position I heard was open. She smiled and directed me to Joel's station. Not wanting to make a fool out of myself, I did not tell him about the rumour Lora shared with me. When I asked if he was looking for a long hair stylist his answer was, "Not at this time but leave your name and number and if we ever have an opening we can call you." I thanked him, and was a little disappointed. I walked away but just as I got to the door, he called out to me, "Wait, what is your name?"

I answered "Chris."

"Do you work for Nora?"

"Yes I do."

"I have been looking for you, we need to talk." He asked, "Can you come back this evening after seven?"

Nodding I said, "Yes I will see you then." My heart was beating so fast I was sure everyone in Windsor could hear and see it skipping. I am sure my feet never touched the ground all the way back to work.

This two-minute dialogue was to be the beginning of my true dream career.

After lengthy discussion options with Ron, we agreed, Nora deserved the courteously of being informed before the grapevine got to her first. Working for Joel was an absolute. A feeling of uneasiness engulfed me. Was this a form of betrayal on my part? Nora had been so very good to me but in all fairness, I brought her a large amount of business.

Nora sensed something was bothering me. Full of emotion I told her about my conversation with Lora and Joel. To my relief and surprise Nora understood, "This does not surprise me dear, I heard from others Joel might be looking for you."Softly she said, "I was hoping it would take a little longer for him to find you though." Sheepishly she added, "If I wasn't so selfish I would have told you he was looking for you."

Feeling guilty about leaving, I offered to stay for two weeks so she could fill my spot. Now there's something you need to understand about the world of hairdressing. Beauticians do tend to move from place to place and most of their clientele follow. Owners dread it when members of their staff move on. This was, however the nature of the beast. In my case, Nora was conscious of Joel's amazing reputation and understood. It was no secret; Nora would have jumped at the chance to work at Wilder Studios herself. She wished me well assuring me I would always be welcomed back. She was sincere; our relationship was always mutually beneficial.

The next day would be my last at Nora's salon. One of our hairdresser's unspoken rules was no one expected to get or to give notice. Bosses were anxious; if clients knew ahead of time they would leave, following the hairdresser to their new location. Their hope was that the customer would get used to another beautician in the shop and stay. That does happen in a small percentage of the cases but it is not the norm. It was bad enough losing staff but losing clientele the sacred cow was harder to deal with. A good hair stylist could make or break a salon and the owners knew this. Nora however had five great hairdressers working for her, so she would be fine.

Nora and the other girls wished me well and I said my good byes. Although I would only be down the street and one block over I knew it was only fair to Nora that I keep my distance. This was my way of making sure any customers wishing to stay at Nora's would not be embarrassed or uncomfortable having to face me. This does happen occasionally. I think because of the closeness sometimes the client feels guilty when they choose for one reason or another not to follow us, maybe they feel like they are cheating on us. I am not sure, as I have never been the customer. Joel's was extremely pricey and I knew there were some clients who would not be able to afford his salon. Plus there were customers who started with Nora's and would prefer the atmosphere there. I was not so wrapped up in myself that I didn't know some of my customers would not follow me but the ones I was certain of were the ones with long hair. I was extremely excited but I knew I would miss my friendships there. Leaving on good terms when at all possible, was a good motto.

Chapter Thirty-Three

It was unbelievable how comfortably I fit into my new position. Within a week Mrs. Knowles and Jenny were just two of my countless clients who established Wilder Studios as their new beauty salon. Joel placed the customary ad in the paper. It advised my customers where to find me.

Van, Joel's colour specialist, focused on colours. There was no colour he couldn't mix, or colour problem he couldn't solve. Joel's own specialty was styling short hair. He perfected haircuts after taking Vidal Sassoon's course in precision cutting. Sandra's knowledge was restricted to wigs and hairpieces. Leana was our backup girl for all services provided in the salon. I excelled in styling long hair, makeup artistry, and colour theory. The stylists who were working here had a 'feel good' work environment, and which complimented one another. There was no competition between any of us. No one was hesitant to ask for, or to give, help. No one ever said, "That's not my job." We prided ourselves on superior customer service, and Joel demanded it. He took all the courses when new information became available. Then he taught us.

In Windsor, we were the pioneers in many fields, introducing new products to our customers. One of those being the portable blow dryer.

Our level of expertise brought with it many perks. Once we worked for Joel for three months, we where assigned our own personal shampoo girl. Our day would start when our first customer came in. We could choose our own vacation time. It took a long time and hard work for me to get to this point. Working for Joel also gave me a respect among other hairdressers in Windsor. It was a wonderful feeling.

***

I had only been at Wilder's for a month when Joel gave me other opportunities as well. His brother Kevin was the owner of Wilder Photo Studios. The studio was in need of a model for their new pictures in their front window. Since I had modeled before, he asked me to pose for his project. That led to my modeling for various hair shows along with Joel's wife Jodie. Joel and staff entered us in the shows held in Toronto, Detroit and Windsor.

By this time, I had short, silver-white hair, instead of the medium length flame red hair to which I had grown accustomed. It was beautiful, and I loved it! Customers and friends complimented me and said I looked like a movie star. The pictures from the photo studio were stunning. I was so very proud of the way I looked. I was now doing more modeling for Kevin for other projects. It was as if I had stepped back in time. I was modeling a great deal of the time now. My picture in Kevin's window was changed often. Ron was proud of me.

A Hairdresser's Diary

Our salon was so well known in Windsor, that we had many visiting entertainers come to us, or we went to them for their makeup and hair needs. This was how I met 'California Smith', a singer/dancer from Los Angeles. I became her personal makeup artist, hairdresser, and friend. She was blonde, statuesque and gorgeous. Her voice was unforgettable. She was very much down to earth, and I didn't feel out of place when people stared at her or wanted her autograph. If anything, she made me feel beautiful and important. She constantly complimented me on my skills as a hairdresser, makeup artist, and model. Once, when I had to go to the Elmwood to pick up Cali, I was mistaken for one of the nightclub dancers. It was a compliment. They were all so beautiful.

There was a time she wanted me to consider working as a model full time. She said, "I can make it happen." I thanked her, but I was happy the way things were. It was better for my family this way. She spent most of her time off with us. She loved the kids and Ron. It was wonderful hanging out with her. I felt very privileged. We were invited to join her at the Elmwood for her show. This was very exciting!

Cali asked me to go on tour to the Orient as her personal stylist. What an honour. The fact I was married with a family made my decision easy, but not quick. I wanted to savour this moment for as long as I could.

Hairdressing was changing and we changed with it. Joel made sure we always had the up-to-date equipment. We learned how to blow hair dry, and then curl it with a curling iron. This was not without its learning curves. Previously we only used curling irons for touch-ups now they were used overall. I for one suffered a few burns along the way. All lengths of hair could be curled like this. It meant less time under the dryer for the client but more work for us. Gradually, dryers would be used less frequently. Many of our older customers still preferred rollers, they felt their styles lasted longer. It would certainly take some of our customers, especially the older ones longer to get used to the changes. We still found some styles and heads of hair that worked better with rollers. They would never go out of style.

Men still did not come into salons during working hours but later when the doors had been locked. We had a fairly large clientele of men who wanted to be pampered the same as women. Barbers did not accommodate those extra needs. Ron however had to get his hair cut when I could do it. I worked strange hours and after work, I was tired. He would come to pick me up and I would cut his hair no matter the time or day. Fast easy and convenient.

Mrs. Silverstein was my last customer for that day. Ron was in the shampoo room getting Mina to wash his hair. Mrs. Silverstein had been a customer of mine for a long time but had never met Ron. As I stepped in front of her to fix her bangs, she grabbed my arm and pulled me down closer to her. Whispering to me, "Is he one of those, you know strange ones?" She very slightly tilted her head sideways towards where Ron was sitting raising her eyebrows.

I whispered, "Strange ones?"

She said, "You know one of those we don't talk about." She was almost mouthing the words now instead of whispering.

I started to laugh to myself. I quietly answered, "You have no idea how strange he is Mrs. Silverstein he is some WEIRD."

"Really?" she said.

"Yep really!" I exclaimed.

186

Just then, Mina called out to me, "Chris your hubby is ready."

The shocked look on Mrs. Silverstein face was priceless. She looked somewhat embarrassed. I leaned down to her and softly said, "Just because he is my hubby doesn't make him less strange or weird" I gently squeezed her shoulder and we both laughed. She thanked me for not making her feel bad.

She said, "No wonder I like you so much you are special." She hugged me on the way out. We never mentioned it again.

I shared this hilarious story with Joel and Jodie. We decided no one else should know, just in case it slipped out one day when Mrs. Silverstein was in. Joel looked at Jodie and laughed, as if they had a special secret to share. After a few moments of belly laughs, Joel said to me, "Remember when you went for the last session at my brother's studio and you felt uncomfortable when he wanted you to wear only a fur wrap?" I nodded, "And I said you could be there naked and he wouldn't be interested in you." Again I nodded, "Well it isn't because you don't look sexy; he is just one of the strange ones." He added, "Ask him he will tell you the same thing."

"So is that why he bleaches his hair and waxes his eyebrows?" I asked.

"Yes" Jodie answered. I had forgotten my conversation with Billie so many years back until this very moment. All of a sudden, I had a hot pain in the pit of my stomach. I really missed him.

Jodie informed us the next morning that we would be accepting appointments for male customers. Joel Wilder's, would now be known as the first unisex salon in Windsor. Joel said his brother and friends were tired of having to manipulate their work, around our hours and schedules. They understood there would be stares, gossip and whispers. They got those anyway. I was confused. I always cut Ron hair while at work it never posed a problem. Fair enough, it was always after hours or just before closing time.

Once it was out to the public that we accepted clients of both sexes, our phones rang off the hook. Not all of our steady customers took the inevitable change with grace. Some of them indicated feeling uncomfortable with a man in the salon including their own husbands. This is something they would have to get used to or move on. Joel asked those who were verbal about their dislike, "How could you allow men to work on your hair, but not allow them to benefit from our services?" Good question?

New doors opened for men now. This would allow them the same access to haircuts and styles, colors and manicures in the salon as women. They should be entitled, to reap the same benefits of massage and hair treatments. As well as hairpieces and wigs that fit properly.

I for one was excited about this new venture. I was not properly prepared for some of the weird phone calls I received over the next few months. One that comes to mind was a guy calling to book an appointment for the first time. He asked, "Do I get one of those blowy jobs after you cut my hair?" Taken back by the remark I quickly hung up the phone. Shaken I went to Joel and after fumbling with the words told him what kind of unorthodox request I received. He laughed uncontrollably, first at my visibly shocked reaction and then because I misunderstood what the guy was asking. "He only wants his hair blown dry after you cut it." Joel teased. Extremely embarrassed, everyone had a hoot at my expense. Me too! From that, day forwards I made sure the words 'BLOW DRY' were used in the proper context.

Men at times still needed barbers but now they had choices. In Windsor, we were changing the words hairdresser or beautician to stylist. We would not be offering shaves, which was still a barber's job. We did do beard trimming and moustache shaping but not full-face shaves.

The other services more men indulged in was the facial. A completely new line of men's skin care products was emerging. Men started to enjoy the pampering women have always had access to. They were willing to pay for the privilege and comfort. The other surprise to me was that men chose to have female stylists work on them. From my own experience, my male customers were even more loyal to me than many of my female customers. I didn't think that was even possible, but they tipped like they were grateful. It was not always the female clientele that didn't like sharing us. We had a few men that didn't like sitting in a waiting room full of women, especially if those women were over the age of forty. Some misinformed men were under the erroneous impression that the salon would be the new one stop dating service. Some stylist also had to deduce the customers who needed our services and those who were chick hunting. I learned how to handle sticky situations. A couple times, I just asked Joel to handle it for me. This move absolutely drove the message home to the client. Those customers were asked not to return to the salon for any reason. Joel was very protective of us and wanted the transition to be smooth and without incident.

Chapter Thirty-Four

Stella was one of my regulars. She asked me to look at the hairpiece her husband Joseph had. He was embarrassed to wear it but was vain enough to feel old and unattractive without it. Joseph knew it looked phoney, "a rat's nest" he would say. Stella said he was uncomfortable sitting in a room full of women. I assured him privacy in our back room if he would came into the shop. He was agreeable and came in the next day. In his hand was a round, brown box housing a piece of hair that looked and smelled like a dead animal. It was dull, ratty and not shaped or cut properly.

First, I asked, "When was the last time you had it cleaned?" Surprised he answered, "I didn't know I was supposed to. When we purchased it there was no instruction on its upkeep." I assumed they had received instructions, but Stella indicated there were none, neither written nor verbal. We mutually agreed to start with a cleaning. I knew it was an extremely expensive hairpiece that was hand woven using human hair. I wanted to make sure Joseph received the best service

191

possible, so I turned this part over to Sandra, our wig expert. She was able to clean it right at the shop. Working with Sandra gave us the wealth of knowledge needed to spot a cheap wig from an expensive one. We were fortunate to have all the paraphernalia needed to work this piece in the salon. In order to make it look natural I would have to fit and cut it so it matched Joseph's face structure and head measurements. All of these extremely important services should have been preformed it was when first purchased. Almost apologetically, he said, "My wife bought it for me at a wig store years ago in the US. It was a Father's Day gift." No wonder it didn't fit properly. Any reputable wig store does all the measurements and fittings.

Sandra told her, "These are normally part of the purchase price."

Stella said, "I wasn't even given the option of bringing Joseph back for a fitting and cut." "Twelve hundred dollars was a lot of money for us, but I was assured no instructions were necessary." Tearfully she stated, "Joseph was so pleased to have hair again and that was what was important to me." Stella sounded regretful for her actions and good intentions;" I trusted the professionals knew what they were talking about." Joseph couldn't believe he was looking at the same hairpiece he had left with me only two days ago. Even the colour was different now that it was clean. I was so thankful for Sandra's expert help. Once I placed it on his head, I was able to measure just how much it needed to be adjusted. It was at least two sizes too large for his head. That was a tremendous size difference especially for something that was supposed to fit snugly.Sandra advised we send it out to for professionally sizing. She was not comfortable removing that much of the hairpiece, which meant a delay of a couple of days. None of this work was inexpensive. They had already spent hundreds of dollars on something he could not wear as it was.

The next week, Joseph returned for the final steps. He was getting eager and excited about the final process. I was curious why Stella was not with him? He said, "I want to surprise her. She has been very upset and embarrassed by her lack of research before spending such a large amount, only to have to spend more." Joseph stated, "Even though I felt ridiculous wearing the piece the way it was, I did it anyway." Sighing he finished with, "I wanted to show Stella how much I appreciated her sweetness."

Once Joseph was in the chair I removed the piece from the box all cleaned and adjusted. Placing it on his head, I reminded him of the picture I asked for of when he had a full head of hair. This request I could tell bewildered him, but he handed it to me anyway. His only request, "Don't make me look like I'm trying to be twenty, I am not." I laughed. Joseph started to panic when I turned him facing away from the mirror, he grabbed my hand and in a whisper said, "Please Chris, make Stella happy." Smiling I said," We will not disappoint either of you." Not missing a beat Sandra and I went from beautician to magician mode. What started as a shaggy looking mess transformed before our very eyes. When we finished no one would have guessed this was not Joseph's own hair. When it came to cutting and styling wigs and hairpieces, I had always cut and styled the pieces or wigs right on the customers head. Most other shops used a mannequin head. I found this was not as first-rate or natural looking. We as humans don't have perfect shaped heads unlike the fake ones. After I finished the cut, I combed his hair the way he used to wear it so many years ago. Now, the moment of truth. As we turned Joseph to face the mirror, he was noticeably emotional. Sandra and I needed no words from Joseph we knew. "Yes, oh yes" he said, "Stella will be pleased."

"Joseph, do you have any questions?" I asked.

"Yes a couple if you don't mind me sounding uninformed?" he said.

"By all means ask away, what I can't answer Sandra can." We both smiled.

"First," he said "I feel like the thing will stay in place no problem right?"

"Right," I said

"Okay, I would like to know if I go dancing, driving in the convertible or sailing will it fall off?"

"Joseph, I would still be careful, but enjoy yourself. If you are concerned about the wind wear a cap," Stella advised.

I added, "You can comb it, mess it, or wear a cap and it is very natural looking, but remember it is still a hairpiece." The answers seemed to satisfy him.

Sandra provided him a written list of proper instructions. I included the name of a place to buy a proper head to put it on when not in use. The box it came in was not sufficient to keep the shape. Most of all, we stressed upon him the necessity to keep it cleaned. It was clear he wanted to give us a hug but it was not his style nor in his comfort zone. He left smiling.

The next morning when I arrived at work, Stella was in the shop waiting for me with a bouquet of roses and a thank you card. She wanted to thank me for making Joseph so happy. I informed her that Sandra's expert assistance was what made it go so flawlessly. With a twinkle in her eyes she said, "We went out dancing last night something he would not do for years. You two have changed him my dear, thank you." I thought she would never stop thanking us. Joel complimented us on a job well done. Sandra and I were pleased, very pleased. Ron seeing the roses and card said, "I am proud of both of you, your customer feels good about himself because of you two." This is how we at Joel's all worked, together.

Chapter Thirty-Five

Many of the guys that came into the shop at first seemed curious. Pampering was something they didn't receive in the basic barbershop. It was not surprising to learn that some customers thought this would be an easy way to meet women. I'm sure some were successful, but many were unpleasantly disappointed. It was only a few short months and we could already see an incredible difference in our versatile clientele. Husbands and wives were coming in together with their children.

One of the common complaints we received from male customers was the price. They were used to paying a barber far less than we charged. Joel always invited them to please, return to their barbers if it was becoming a hardship. He explained to them we were not barbers but stylists. Not many, but some even tried experimenting with colour rinses to tone down their grey. Amazingly, just that small change could make a devastating difference in one's confidence. Many men didn't want the distinguished look just yet.

We as hairdressers, also evolved to new and exciting heights. Experimenting with new techniques for coloring, cutting and perms, we changed the whole perspective of hairdressing. The bouffant and heavy backcombing trend was coming to an end. We now back brushed, which gave the same effect and lift but not so much tatting of the hair. No more heavy lacquers, instead the hair sprays had gotten lighter with a softer hold. Wash and wear cuts seemed to be the way to go. Haircuts that customers could manage on their own without weekly up keep, were a popular request. The way of cutting hair, our scissors and other utensils changed. Scissors became shorter, smaller and lighter. Even my long haired customers wanted softer and more flowing styles, not so rigid and stiff looking. Colours now came in a huge range, more vibrant, saucy and easier to use. Bleaching was not so harsh looking. Streaking could be done several different ways, foils, hair painting, wide streaks, and thin streaks in multiple colours and shading, the examples go on and on. Hairdressing was far from being boring. We upgraded our knowledge and training all the time.

If there was something new and exciting, Joel's Salon had it first. Sometimes the US had information before Canada did, so Joel and Jodie picked up information at the hair shows in Detroit. It would not be unheard of to find their names in the newspaper the next week. They would be sharing the new and exciting projects we at Joel's would be involved in next. I was proud to be associated with this wonderful family and this salon. Ron felt comfortable in the presence of all the stylists too. Unlike Carmen's, there was not the same camaraderie after work or the constant bringing in of food and such, but the feeling of belonging was there.

A Hairdresser's Diary

Everyone at Joel's had respect for one another and showed it. There was never any competition on who could do a better job or who worked more or who made the most money. We all worked together, even Joel. If one of us was behind, he would not think twice to step in and give us a hand. These things we all did without a second thought. Respect is what we gave and respect is what we received.

This was my first Christmas (1969) at Joel's. In other shops I had been exceptionally busy for the holidays, but I was not prepared for the next two weeks. Two weeks before Christmas we had a meeting. Each of us was encouraged to share our years of insight concerning dos and don'ts, for customer and stylist alike. Jodie would post them for everyone to see so there could be not mistakes or misunderstandings. I shared my rule of NO cut, perms, colours or extras the days of Christmas and New Years. Everyone voted for that one. Joel wanted NO walk ins under any circumstances. Not that we would have time, but occasionally, a regular customer would bring someone from out of town and want us to fit them in. This was not fair, as we would get behind making it unfair for everyone else. Therefore, that rule passed. Van wanted us to have two more girls hired to help with shampoos, waiting on customers and cleaning up. This way we as stylists could concentrate on hair only. We would all chip in to help pay, but Joel had two nieces that would do it for tips. That was settled. I had already notified my longhaired customers about my night before rule, but most already knew from previous years.

The area of town that Joel's salon was in and his contacts for several of his charities made his clientele mostly of the Jewish faith. Joel told us not to bring anything to eat on those busy days.

He said, "You will be sampling some of the best traditional foods in town brought to us by our clients." This was a tradition in his salon, which started some years back by his customers.

We worked the two days before making sure we had everything we would need and at our fingertips. Joel closed the shop at noon the day before, as we needed to be at work for six thirty the next morning. Our last appointment was booked for ten that night. That meant we would be walking out the door not much before eleven thirty, if we were lucky. Only to do it again the next week end for New Years Eve.

When I dragged myself into the house at almost midnight, I was in tears. I don't think I ever worked so hard in all my years. With me, I had a large box in my hands. Ron asked what was in it? I told him I didn't have time to look yet. Jodie suggested that any gifts brought for us by our customers, be placed in a box with our names on it and therefore they would not get in the way. When we left, she handed us our box to take home. I was far too tired to open any of the gifts that night. After we had our Christmas, just the four of us, I had another with all the lovely gifts from thankful, generous and satisfied clients. Mrs. Silverstein, Joseph and Stella, and Jenny were just a few names that where found on those gifts. The feeling was wonderful and satisfying.

New Years was a different story, the clients showered us not with gifts but with money. The same wonderful variety of food still flowed and the day was even more hectic and crazy busy. I went home even more tired than I did at Christmas, if that was possible. When I walked in the door of our apartment, it was one minute to midnight. Ron learned early on, that New Years Eve was not one of the nights we would be out celebrating. This night, however, was one to be celebrated. Not having the time to stop for even a minute the whole day, I also didn't have time to check my smock pockets. When I emptied them, Ron and I could hardly believe our eyes. Lying on the table in crumpled, folded, and rolled bills was seven hundred dollars. I had not one coin. Some of the bills were twenties. I could not believe what I was seeing. That was more than I made in a month. I was flabbergasted and Ron and I both gave thanks. This was so much more than I ever expected, and I was proud that I was able to make my customers feel I was worth so much to them. This was a Christmas and New Years I would never forget and Joel said it was like that every year so just enjoy.

.

Chapter Thirty-Six

I t was June 1970. Jodie and Joel had been on one of their trips to Detroit to attend a beauty products seminar. It was while they had been away, that Ron and I received the overwhelming, heartbreaking news from our doctor. I lost the precious baby I was carrying. Ron and I were devastated, our hearts felt broken. Our doctor advised us to go away for a few days, first because I needed to rest, and secondly, we needed time to absorb and come to terms with our loss. Thank God, we didn't need to explain to Christine and Terry, both too young to understand.

Van had taken over while Joel was away. Therefore, after explaining to him our need to grieve, he gave me a week off work. Ron was owed a week's vacation that he took. After informing my concerned and understanding customers, we made our plans. On our way out the door, Van called out to me, "Have an accident" I answered back, "Okay we will," and I waved goodbye.

Little did I know that is exactly what would happen! On our way home from our five day bereavement time, we had a destructive, life altering, car accident that dramatically changed the rest of our lives. We were involved in a hit and run accident. The driver who sideswiped us was drunk. Our car was totalled. The damage to my back would be horrific and permanent. With no seatbelts at the time, I was sitting with my feet on the hump between the driver and passenger. My left arm was draped over the back of my seat. I was turned facing Ron and my knees were resting against the front of the seat. After the accident, my body was so badly twisted that my forehead hit the passenger side window. My knees remained leaning against the seat. Ron thankfully sustained no injuries.

***

My life would never again be the same. Our family as a whole would suffer the consequences from the stupidity of one man's brainless decision to drink and drive. I was hospitalized for several weeks before being sent home.

The first week in hospital Van came to see me. He was crying and kept saying, "I am so very sorry. It was only a joke. I didn't mean it." He repeated that over and over again. I assured him, I knew he meant no harm. An unfortunate horrible accident that left me scared, in excruciating pain, and very worried. When he left, he placed a pretty pink housecoat on the bed. He had picked it out himself to show his concern.

My stay in hospital was lengthy and the only people allowed to visit me at the time were family. Ron needed to work and I had no one else close by. We had just lost our baby now this. Neither of us could understand why we had so much to deal with all at once. Thank God, we had each other to lean on.

Things were becoming more than we could bear. Ron was worried when he could not be with me during some of the painful tests I had to go through. We could not afford both of us off work.

Ron's oldest sister stepped in and took our children to her house to care for them. My mother was still trying to find away to take them with her, but Ron was not comfortable with those arrangements. We were still estranged to some degree. He did not want them so far from his eagle eye; at least his sister would bring them to see him once a week.

One day to my delight, I was surprised to hear my mother was in the waiting room, awaiting permission to see me. I was shocked, when my visitor turned out to be Mrs. Silverstein. When I went to say some thing, she put her finger up to her lips and shushed me. The nurse left and she said," I talked to Ron today and he said only family could come to see you. I know your mother can not be here, so I said I was your mother." My tears showed my appreciation. She sat on the side of my bed and let me cry in her arms as if I was her little girl. She played my mother every weekday for the whole month of my hospitalization. I was so thankful for her good heart and kindness. She would massage my back, shave my legs, help with my hair, all the things a mother would do. She brought fresh baked goods and prepared dishes for Ron to make his life easier. Ron said, "Honey, she is a godsend for both of us"

I was devastated when she passed away. I was not able to go to the funeral with Ron. I was home but bedridden. Not once did she let me know how sick she was, in all the time she came to mother me. I felt guilt ridden that I wasn't there for her. Ron said in a way I was. She had no children, so lovingly, in her own way she adopted me.

When I was able to have visitors I was amazed how many of my customers and fellow hairdressers visited. Some I am sure came out of curiosity, most really cared like Nora. We both cried. She said, "I tried several times to come visit you but I wasn't allowed." I told her about how well Mrs. Silverstein took such good care of me. She said, "I feel better knowing someone was here for you."

Although pain was my constant companion, I worried about my family feeling as if I had abandoned them. There was no way of knowing just yet, how much damage was done to my back or how long I would be away from home or out of work. It could be months or years. It turned out to be two years.

***

Once out of hospital I was confined strictly to an orthopaedic mattress on my living room floor. Having two children one five the other two, no car, me having no job, Ron had to hitch hike to work every morning and home again at night. Once home he took care of all household and family duties. This demanding pace day after day took its toll on him. At the age of twenty-three, he suddenly became father, mother, caregiver, sole supporter, housekeeper, cook, and nurse. During the day, we had a homemaker but she did as little as possible. Never once did I hear 'the love of my life' complain about the devastating conditions we were in. Not only did he shoulder this horrendous burden on his young shoulders he had to do it alone. Neither his nor my parents offered any support, emotionally, physically or financially. We were on our own and had to fend for ourselves.

A Hairdresser's Diary

The living room floor was my home one hundred percent of the time for seven long and painful months. Ron jokingly was heard to say," I remember the love honour and obey part of the marriage ceremony but where did it say empty the bed pan?"

Our two year old son, had never seen me stand for all those months. He played on the floor beside me and therefore he never found it necessary to get up and walk. In fact, he could crawl faster than most kids could walk at his age.

After my first surgery, and a three-month stay in hospital I arrived home in a full back brace. Terry took one look at me and started to scream, he was afraid to come near me. At first, I could not understand Ron pointed out our son's fear stemmed from several months of not seeing me in an upright position. Now it made sense, once I got down on his level and he stopped crying and ran to me. Just one more obstacle added to our already problematical life. I now needed several months of therapy to help me walk again. I had not been on my feet for months now.

The drunk driver had no insurance. Therefore, there was no immediate help for us. The charges against him were hit and run, driving without a license, failing to meet terms of probation, driving drunk, driving a stolen car, driving without insurance, and dangerous driving. The courts ordered him back to jail he was a career criminal, and we were left high and dry. The only insurance available to us was through the governments, "unsatisfied judgment", which meant no help, benefits, or much needed relief for us. The rest of our lives would dramatically change. We hired an attorney. He got us the maximum amount allowed under unsatisfied judgment. It was, to say the least; hopelessly inadequate to compensate me for the loss of my career. The chronic pain I would live with for the rest of my life and the suffering of my family went uncompensated as well. The loss of my wages made us financially strapped and we could not keep up. There was no relief in sight.

Almost a year had passed (1971) since the first surgery and I was just starting to get up and about when I needed back surgery again. This time to fix the mistakes the first doctor made and remove debris left behind from the surgery. I had not been getting better.

My mother and stepfather had finally come to visit. They convinced us they would ask the family to gather enough funds to help us buy an inexpensive car. The help never came. After much begging and pleading, Ron's mom finally lent us the money for a five hundred dollar car but only after, she took a lien out on it. The fact that we were so young and moved away from London did not sit well in her craw. It was at this time we knew we were totally on our own. The only outside help we ever received was Ron's older sister and his older brother's family who helped take care of our two children while I was in hospital.

It was impossible for Ron to make ends meet on his pay alone and even though we were in litigation for the accident, we could get no other help. Finally, between our lawyer and my doctors we moved back to Windsor, but into geared to income housing. Ron was a very proud man and begrudgingly he accepted the help. I was feeling guilty and useless. I always made good money, and now I was only causing the family hardship. I was so medicated I didn't know what was happening much of the time.

Chapter Thirty-Seven

Two years later (July 1972), I recovered as well as could be expected and I decided to go back to work part time. My doctors advised against it, but I had to try. We were desperate. I knew I could not go back to Joel's. It had been over two years since I had seen him. Not having any idea how long I might be able to continue working posed a problem. I needed to find a job that was very part time, working only nights and weekends. This way Ron could be home to care for the kids.

Lady luck and my Guardian Angel were with me. While shopping at the Devonshire Mall, I noticed an ad in the window of the beauty salon for a part time receptionist. Rose, the owner of the salon, hired me immediately. Starting at the reception desk taking and managing appointments, would be easier on my back. The wages would be significantly less than I had enjoyed while working at Joel's. Our only concern was to do whatever it took to help our family survive. 'Welfare was not in our vocabulary.' Living in Windsor housing was a hand up, not a hand out, and we would use it that way. We knew that fifty percent of my wages no matter how small would have to go back to the City of Windsor. The remainder would be our ticket out of Windsor housing. I was well aware of the pain I would have to endure and Ron knew his job would not end at five each day. We would do whatever it took to make this work. "That which does not kill us makes us stronger," was the motto we tried to live by. Believe me; we had already had our share of tests. We prayed and prayed that soon a settlement would come and reimburse us for our losses.

Ron was excited about my new job. The relief on his face was immediately noticeable. I felt that finally I was able to take some of the load from his overburdened shoulders. My hours would be Thursday and Friday nights from six until nine and Saturday ten until four. I started the very next evening.

The salon decor was in light greens, bright yellows and white. Everything was very bright and colourful. The first night I was there, I had a bright idea. We were all girls working in the salon. I suggested we all have matching hot pants outfits, accented with knee high white boots. It was all the rage and style. Rose and the girls thought this would be grand. We had matching outfits custom made. We looked amazing and everywhere we went in the mall, people immediately knew where we worked Rose was pleased with the free advertisement.

One month into my new job Marne, a former customer, walked by the salon and noticed me at the desk. After a couple hugs and a few minutes of catching up, she asked, "Chris will you do my hair for my daughter's wedding?" I explained that I was hired only to manage appointments. My doctor's strict orders advised that I not stand on my feet for long periods. She pleaded, "Please just this once." Almost in tears, she begged, "Chris, I will never ask again but this is my daughter's wedding. Please!!" I

promised I would pass it by Rose and if she said okay, I would
Rose was delighted. She had been trying to get me to let her
advertise my whereabouts making it easier for my previous clients
to find me. I always said, "No." I wanted to, but my doctor was
against putting the added stress on my back. The risk of not
being able to work at all scared me. I was on a great deal of pain
meds at the time. By the time I got home, it was all I could do to
walk properly the pain was excruciating. I needed the extra time
between workdays to recoup my strength.

As you could guess, it was not long before I was doing
hair more often than not. Rose even hired another shampoo girl.
"All you have to do is hair no extras," she would say.

Brian was one of my new regular customers. He was also
the manager of the mall's bank. He came in once a week for a
shampoo and monthly for a haircut. One visit he asked, "Are you
up to taking care of six of my buddies next Friday night? I would
only work from six to nine Friday nights, which would work out
perfectly.

When I arrived to the salon that night Rose, with a
mischievous grin said, "Chris, you have some customers waiting
for you in the shampoo room Leah isn't in to do your shampoos
so I will do them for you." Thinking this rather strange I thanked
her. There I found reclining at the shampoo basins six guys, really
big guys, dressed in expensive leather with heavy chains, leather
boots, tattoos and more.

"May I help you guys?" I asked timidly.

The biggest of them replied, "No thanks, we are waiting
for Chris."

I took a deep breath not knowing what to expect next
and said, "I am Chris".

The guys laughed, "Brian sent us but didn't tell us you were a chick."

Nervously laughing I bantered back, "Last time I looked I wasn't a guy." The ice was broken and we laughed together. I asked, "Are you still wanting hair cuts even if I am a chick?"

One of them answered, "Whoever Brian gets that's who we want."

To be honest I was a little intimidated. Okay! A lot intimidated by this group of motorcyclists. Especially when I had learned, they were from a local gang. Not often does one hear good things about gangs. I had never heard about gangs until I moved to London. I was only sixteen and the rumours caused me to be fearful.

You know the saying 'never judge a book by its cover?' Well that certainly was the rule in this case I never met more perfect gentlemen. Leo, (Lion) was a dentist; Frank, (Frankie) was a salesman for a large car company. The biggest and boldest was Brian's regional manager Craig, (Banger). I would never have guessed, there were so many professionals in a motorcycle gang. Then there was of course Brian, the banker. As I explained they were dressed in leathers. Tonight was their bi monthly club night. I apologized as I explained my first impression. They laughed because Leo said, "How could this young chick know how to cut men's hair?" "Maybe we should beg out." One of them said. Another mentioned a magazine that might benefit from my sexy presence. We laughed, discussing everything from families to motorcycles. My total knowledge on cyclists was zero. It was very interesting. They answered my questions about their clubs and explained why they wore leather. Surprisingly, I was pleased to find that they really made a huge contribution to communities.

My attitude took a complete U-turn. No longer was I apprehensive or frightened to be in the company of these men. Fear of the unknown is our worst enemy. Next time Brian came in, he said his friends were impressed with me and my skill and they would be back. These six guys were the biggest tippers I ever had. I was the brunt of titillating teasing about my six-biker friends by the other staff. Flippantly I told them they were just jealous of my new bodyguards.

Chapter Thirty-Eight

By now, it was widespread news that men frequented beauty salons. One night, Rose had a male customer come in for makeup instructions. She was a little surprised, but we were there to provide a service no matter what their gender. It turned out this person enjoyed wearing his wife's clothes and makeup when she was out, but was too embarrassed to ask her for lessons. Was this strange? Not really. A little different maybe. This was to be the beginning of new and unusual situations for us as hairdressers. I recall the young man who came to get his hair streaked after a day of house painting. His boyfriend liked the painted look. I received a call from one gentleman who wanted to know what bra size he might need. After I informed him we didn't sell bras, he quickly hung up.

The fact we worked at the mall brought with it some unusual questions. I for one, tried very hard not to react unkindly or unsympathetically to any ones odd requests. Although at times, it was difficult to keep a straight face. When a client asked to have only half his head shaved and make up applied to only half his face that raised eyebrows. All sorts of visions went through my head. He could see the questions in my eyes and shared, "I am playing half man, half woman in a stage play." Sighing, he said, "Two other salons turned me down." Adding, "They thought I was a prankster. I could have explained but it was none or their business. You didn't ask, therefore I don't mind telling you. I appreciate that you didn't snicker like the others." How could I tell this trusting person that on the inside I WAS chuckling.

Regular requests for manicures, massage, facials (without makeup), colours, haircuts and styling made it obvious that men found their place in the beauty salon.

Rose decided to add the new gel acrylic nail service to the salon. This was something that tweaked my interest and I could sit therefore, it took some pressure off my back. Wow! I was not prepared for the nose burning, mind-numbing odour. The strong, overwhelming acetone smell, literally took my breath away. I certainly could understand the instructions for it to be used only in a well-ventilated room. It was almost impossible to accommodate the instructions 'to use in well-ventilated areas' in the confines of our mall space. If you have ever smelled airplane glue, just multiply that twenty times, and it is pretty close to the odour of the acrylic gel. The shop next to ours complained so we finally discontinued the service.

Rose had a huge walk-in business due to our mall location. It was not unheard of to have a customer, who played hairdresser, expect us to fix their mess. At times, it was an easy fix, sometimes there was no hope. As I once stated, "We are only beauticians not magicians."

Many of the mishaps consisted of excessively butchered haircuts. Some of the problems where easily fixed. Unless of course you are the customer whose children, ages seven and five, felt they should play hairdresser with daddy's electric razor. Oh my, this was truly a hairdresser's nightmare. The little boy was easy. I just gave him a brush cut, but the little girl was a different story. Her lovely long, blonde, curly hair had pieces missing all over her head. The only thing that saved her from absolute disaster was the length of her hair. This prevented the razor from touching her scalp. When I told her we needed to cut her hair, she wrapped her arms around her head shaking it violently back and forth screaming. It was obvious she wanted her long hair no matter what it looked like. Not getting any closer to fixing the mess, I needed to conjure up another plan. I knew this was going to take a great deal of patience and imagination I suggested to her, that maybe we could create her very own special hair cut, together. I promised not to cut her hair until she was ready. This worked like a charm; I was able to influence her thinking to create an image in her head that I knew was achievable. Her mother told her she could brag to her friends that she had her own custom designed haircut. Not needing more kid disasters, I asked this to be kept our secret. One disadvantage of being a hairdressing parent is always having scissors handy; our kids like to mimic us. Oops, happens to us as well we just don't need to pay someone else to fix the problems.

During a rainstorm, a lady came running into our shop, right to the back towards the shampoo sinks. She was holding a wet paper grocery bag over her head. Rose followed her to see what was happening. After removing the saggy paper bag, we saw black streaks running down her face. She had used a black, store brand, tint on her hair and had not washed it out properly, so when it got wet the black residue ran down her face. She looked like the back end of a skunk. Thank goodness, she came in when she did. If it had ran into her eyes she could have become blind. Shampooing the extra color from her hair was easy, but the black run marks on her face would take a couple of days to dissipate.

I had one customer who was so tall she had to bending over the sink forwards so we could wash her hair. Another customer was too large to fit in the regular size chair and was angry with us for not supplying equipment for the larger built person. She pointed out the booster chair for children, the pump up chairs for short people, but the lack of oversized chairs. I did not have an answer. As far as I could remember no matter what salon I worked in, the chairs were always the same size.

Some customers used their hair time to unwind, while spouses or other family members shopped. Pampering was a luxury we all deserved. If you take a moment to think what is enjoyable about going to the hairdresser, you might be surprised at your answer. How much trust do you place in your hairdresser's knowledge and techniques? Have you ever told your hairdresser something you might hesitate to tell a friend or family member? The answer to this question ninety -nine percent of the time is yes. We cultivate trust, which comes in all forms. To abuse that is unforgivable.

Rose, was having financial problems so she brought Vito to work in the salon. He was the first male Rose had ever hired. When he started to push me around, I did not pay much attention to his bossiness, thinking it was just another macho thing. He would bark orders at me to clean up after him or do his shampoos, or clean up his station. The constant harassment from his bossiness and disgusting sexual remarks, upset me. I could not understand why Rose permitted it. I found out after two weeks of harassment, he was to be our new boss. No one was happy about this. Rose explained she would lose the shop if she did not bring in a partner. I suggested she might lose her business anyway, as everyone would end up quitting.

The last straw for me came one evening. I was leaving for home and Vito asked me for a ride to the bus stop. I reluctantly agreed. We got into the car and he immediately started making crude remarks. He talked about how hot, wonderful and sexy he was, and any woman that would with him would never ever go back to their partner. Vito said once experiencing him; I would never want my husband again. He was vulgar! He refused to get out of the car at the bus stop, instead; he demanded I drive him home, which was out of my way. He threatened me with the loss of my job if I did not obey. I continued driving. The urge to wipe the smirk off his face with the back of my hand was overwhelming. I was thoroughly disgusted. I was not as afraid of losing my job as I was of him. I desperately needed to find a way out of this situation and fast.

Angrily, I drove into my own driveway; I ran into the house and screamed to Ron, "Get him out of our car!" Ron furiously stomped outside and demanded, "Vito get out of our car right now!" he continued with, "I called a cab for you." As Vito was getting out of the car, he swore at Ron and threatened to fire me. We watched from a safe distance out the front window until the cab picked him up. After his vivid threats, I was convinced Vito would retaliate.

I did not return to Rose's shop, instead, I called her. I explained the situation and told her I would no longer work for her, as long Vito was there. She was furious with me and said, "I need Vito, it is the only way I can keep the salon." She went on to tell me how ungrateful I was for all she had done for me. I felt bad for her, but there was no way in hell, I was going to be in the same room with that ignorant person. I apologized and wished Rose all the best.

I soon heard through the grapevine, Vito no longer was a partner and Rose no longer owned the salon. The sad news held no consolation to me. Rose deserved better. Rose, soon called me to apologize and ask me back. Even though she no longer owned the shop, she was the new manager. I could not in good conscience trust her judgment again. Thanking her for her offer, I politely declined. She reminded me of all the special things she did for me, which she would not have done for others. I reminded her of all the business I brought to her and the piece de resistance, Vito.

Chapter Thirty-Nine

I no longer had the ideal job. The idyllic hours without suffering too much pain just ended. I was upset at having to search once again. How would I get something that fit our schedule as well as this job did? Ron assured me with my proven reputation, I would not be out of work long. I had been working long enough I could apply for unemployment insurance, but there was a catch. Because I quit, I did not qualify. I decided that I would make my case in person. After explaining my situation and reasons for quitting, I was accepted. What a relief.

Unhappily, it was very close to Christmas. I was hoping this year would be different from the last three. I was crafty and was able to make most of my gifts. Our children had not been raised to be 'gimme' kids. They loved to make and receive homemade things. From the time Christine was three we had our own Christmas tradition. I would find an empty box round if possible, and glue cotton all around the outside. On the inside I would place very inexpensive items; dinky cars, candy bars, or silly erasers, to list a few. These items where tied with a very long ribbon that would hang on the out side of the box. Each child had a different coloured ribbon. For twelve nights before bed, the kids would draw one of their ribbons. I called this a 'Snowball.' The kids looked forward to this every year and it was something their friends did not have. This tradition passed to our granddaughter and now our grandson. We hoped this Christmas would be better but now I had no job and no word of a settlement either.

Ron was not angry. He would not see me back in that poisonous environment with Vito. We would make do we always did. The good Lord would once again hear my prayers and He would guide us down the right path. We never asked Him to take care of things for us. We only asked, for guidance to do it ourselves.

I decided that until I was able to resume my career, I would offer my services from home to friends and family. I could call some of my clients from the mall I already did the hair of a few of my neighbours. The few dollars from a haircut or two always was enough for milk and bread.

I didn't have the chance to make those calls. A sales rep from a beauty supply company told Nora I was no longer working. Through gossip, she would have already known I had been working at the mall. The incident with Vito would be spreading like wildfire.

Surprisingly, Nora took the opportunity to call, and offered me my old job back. After all these years, she still wanted me! I talked about the loss of our baby, the car accident, surgeries and my limitations, as well as my doctor's concerns. She sympathetically replied, "None of that matters, we will work around all of those things." We agreed I would work Thursday and Friday nights for three hours and four hours on Saturdays. This would be perfect. Ron was ecstatic. The notion of working for Nora again was exhilarating. An ad would be placed in the Windsor Star, advertising my whereabouts, and days and hours of operation. The good news, I had not been unemployed long enough to even collect my first unemployment cheque. Ron laughed, "I told you so honey." We both gave thanks and cried with relief.

It is somewhat strange when you have been away from a place for a while and go back. Things looked different but still the same. This is how I found it at Nora's. We had a wonderful first night, mostly chatting and catching up. She said, "When you left Joel's many of your customers came back here. They couldn't connect with the girl hired to take your place." Saying with a smile, "Many said it was not the same without you." I was flattered. My customers had a great place to go back to and now I was back as well. I thanked her repeatedly for giving me this second chance. She laughed saying, "No dear, thank you. I would have done the exact same thing; I never held that against you. Deep down though I was wishing you would find Joel's too much and come back." Sighing she said," I think you would have preferred different circumstances though right?" Smiling I nodded.

We talked about the ad she would put in the paper. "Do you think my old clientele will remember me?"

"Are you kidding you have always been remembered" I was not able to convince Nora, to skip the expense of an ad. The length of time I would be able to continue working made no difference to her. My pain would be my barometer. Still she was willing hire me on even if it was for a short time. We knew customers that came back to me would stay this time if I asked them to. I was still the only hairdresser she had that styled long hair the way I could. The flood of phone called we received in the next three weeks made my head swim. My working hours were fully booked and I never had an empty place in my appointment book. The girls that I worked with before where still all there and welcomed me back. I felt at home.

Jenny was back even though she had been in touch with me the whole time, I was off I had been doing her hair at my home. Until now that is. I insisted those customer had to come to the salon when I was working. I knew I could not work at home and the salon too. It was too much stress on my back.

***

It was like old home week. How incredible was this? Even customers from the mall found me. I did miss my motorcycle friends. Brian called to explain it was not advisable for them to come to downtown Windsor. Their presence and leather gear might cause uneasiness for others.

Nora wanted me to work more hours. My customer base was growing in leaps and bounds. I was not able to accommodate her. I was already feeling the extra pain in my back and legs. She backed off.

Chapter Forty

N ow (1973) after almost four, long, life-altering years of suffering, we were advised of the mere pittance of a settlement due us. It was such a small amount due to government insurance regulations. The perpetrator that ruined our lives had no other insurance. After all the deductions, lawyer's fees, hospitalization repayment and other expenses, my compensation for the ruin of the rest of my life was less than five-thousand dollars. I went through so many surgeries and was in constant pain. Somehow I felt cheated. I would get angry when I heard stories of others who received enormous settlements for just a fanny tap. Struggling through so much made our family closer. Ron and I decided that if we were to get our lives back in order we needed to put this pittance to good use. We knew that nothing would give me back my career or what our family suffered or for the pain in years to come. Ron and I made the decision to use the money to make the family's life more comfortable. We now had a valid reason for excitement we decided to build our first house, small, but cozy, and ours. Everyone at the shop was pleased for us.

Ron and I were delighted. I was pregnant again. Although, afraid of losing another child we could still feel joy. This affected my back and the pain was far worse. I was constantly having premature labour and had to have the contractions medically stopped.

Finally when I was seven months pregnant the doctors advised me to let them deliver my very preemie baby. Doug was finally born (July 4th) but not without several health issues. Within the first twenty-four hours, his doctor informed me he would probably not survive. Ron and I could hardly speak for weeping. Not again please, God, not again, two losses were enough. I had surgery the next day to remove my tubes. This meant no more pregnancies. When I recovered in a few days I was able to go home but not without my little precious little bundle of joy. He was too tiny and sick to leave the hospital.

I had not even been allowed to touch him yet. The nurse seeing us on the other side of the nursery glass motioned to us to stay where we were. She came out of the nursery, took me by the arm and handed me a gown and mask. I looked at Ron and the nurse said, "I am sorry dear but the doctor said only the mommy and only for a couple minutes." With tears in his eyes, Ron gently pushed me toward the nursery door. "Honey, go I will be right here watching." So excited my heart raced, I sat in the rocking chair beside the incubator Doug was in. As I sat there, I was sure my heart would explode. Then gently the nurse placed him in my arms. Sobs broke from my throat. I was warned not to move him or to even kiss him. The tubes attached to his tiny body made it crucial to keep him still. Two minutes was my limit. In one way, it felt like time stood still and in another it seemed to speed past. Through blurred and teary eyes, I looked up and smiled at Ron, who was crying as well. Grief-stricken we had to leave our sweet wee one there, along with part of our hearts. Ron and I went home empty handed.

Nora gave me the time I needed. Five weeks later we brought Doug home weighing a whole five pounds. What was even more memorable about his homecoming was we were bringing him home to our new house. We had a new baby and a new home. Ron also had just received a sales promotion for the welding company he worked for and his first company car. Could things be any better?

My customers now comfortable with the staff at Nora's, all was coming together. Then, the oddest thing happened. While I was unpacking, I found the notes from the psychic customer I serviced at Nora's salon. I read and reread them.

Here they are. Today I had a customer who said she was a psychic; she predicted we would have five children. I had three children but five pregnancies. She said, I would come into a fair sum of money but I would have to suffer for it. A fair amount was barely enough for a small down payment on a one level house. As far as suffering, she understated that one. Does a severe car accident, several surgeries and living with chronic pain for the rest of my life constitute suffering?

She stated by the time I was twenty-eight my life would change forever I was only twenty-five when my life had been altered forever.

The last prediction was I would not be working for Nora by the time I was twenty-eight. If she meant the change I made to Joel's she was off by a few years. As far as I knew, I was still working for her so I think she missed that one. I guess she was partially correct it was just sad it had to come true this way.

I balled the piece of paper up and threw it in the garbage. It was too spooky for me to keep. To this day, I have never allowed anyone else to predict my future even for fun.

Chapter Forty-One

It was October 1973, and I had only been back to work for a few months when my back seized and I was unable to move. My customer's hair was so long I could not reach the bottom without almost sitting on the floor. I requested she allow one of the other girls to blow dry it for her but she said, "I pay extra to have you do it Chris so that is what I expect." I should have stood my ground. When I tried to stand up, the pain was agonizing and crippling. Nora called an ambulance to take me to emergency. That marked the last day I would ever work in a beauty salon. I was only twenty-eight. The last prediction from the psychic just came true. Goose bumps covered my body as chills radiated from head to toe.

Nora, visited me almost daily in hospital and was genuinely concerned; she expressed her gratitude for all the business, I brought back to her. She showed her appreciation for the training I gave the girls in the colour theory business which was still flourishing for sharing my techniques for long hair styling and especially for being her friend. This was a devastating and sad moment. We cried knowing there would never be another day at Nora's for me. While working, I asked each of my clients to choose another stylist that they felt connected to and to stay at Nora's if I ever had to leave. They were more than happy to do that customers do not want to change salons if possible either.

More hospitalization, surgery and treatment were in store for my future. The doctors advised me I would never be able work again. This devastating news left me depressed and deeply saddened. Twenty-eight years old and my whole life from now on would begin with either chronic or disabled. God was my daily whipping post for the next few months. I begged Him, promised Him, swore at Him, and prayed to Him sometimes all at once, until I had none of those feelings left inside me. Confused and bewildered there was no way I could understand how the inexcusably careless actions of one drunk driver could ruin the lives of so many in one family. Hairdressing was the only career I ever dreamed of and the only job I knew how to do. It was painfully obvious my modeling days had ended too.

I would have to find a way to keep my hand in my craft when the dust settled and things calmed down. As I once said, hairdressing was in my blood so I needed to find a way to continue feeding my addiction and in time, I would.

About the Author

I am a 67-year-old woman who lives in Paris Ontario, Canada. I have three wonderful, amazing children, two sons-in-law, and one daughter-in-law who are just like my own. I brag about my grandchildren, a twenty-seven-year-old granddaughter and a seven-year-old grandson. Ron and I were married at nineteen and have been married forty-eight interesting and adventurous years.

A severe car accident caused by a drunk driver took my livelihood away and left me to live the rest of my life with chronic pain. Until then I was a successful hairdresser, make-up artist and a model. To help deal with the pain, I taught myself to paint. First on clothing, then walls, wooden pieces, stone, and now on canvas.

It came as a surprise after telling my hairdressing stories for the millionth time that my son-in-law suggested I write about them. I have been writing poetry for as long as I can remember, but writing a story was foreign to me.

http://ahairdressersdiaries.wordpress.com/